IN PRAISE OF FAMOUS
HORSES

Sean Magee is the author of many books on matters equine, including *Ascot: The history* (2002); *Lester's Derbys* (2004), with Lester Piggott; and *Arkle: The story of the world's greatest steeplechaser* (2005). He is also author of the history of *Desert Island Discs* (2012).

IN PRAISE OF FAMOUS
HORSES

An A–Z of the Most Celebrated in History
and Culture, Myth and Sport

SEAN MAGEE

WEIDENFELD & NICOLSON

First published in Great Britain in 2020 by Weidenfeld & Nicolson
This paperback edition published in 2022 by Weidenfeld & Nicolson
an imprint of The Orion Publishing Group Ltd
Carmelite House, 50 Victoria Embankment
London EC4Y 0DZ

An Hachette UK Company

1 3 5 7 9 10 8 6 4 2

A CIP catalogue record for this book
is available from the British Library.

ISBN (Mass Market Paperback) 978 1 4746 1911 0
ISBN (eBook) 978 1 4746 1081 0
ISBN (Audio) 978 1 4746 2034 5

Printed in Great Britain by Clays Ltd, Elcograf, S.p.A

www.orionbooks.co.uk

Preface

From D.H. Lawrence's horse Aaron, whose hide was posthumously recycled as a duffel bag, to Zippy Chippy, fabled American loser who became a national celebrity, each of the horses featured in this book has a claim to fame.

Some – among them Black Beauty, Bucephalas, Champion the Wonder Horse, Phar Lap, Mister Ed, Rocinante – are permanent residents of the equine pantheon.

Others have to settle for notoriety: horses such as Rossa Prince and Mister Chippendale, point-to-pointers who have the unusual distinction of failing to win a walkover.

It has been estimated that the horse population of the world is around 75 million, and there must be nearly the same number of books on equestrian matters. The reason for adding the current volume to the already groaning bookshelf is simple: to celebrate horses who for whatever reason have made themselves famous.

We salute famous winning racehorses and famous losing racehorses; mythical horses and military horses; literary and historical horses; operatic, television and movie horses.

A word of warning. This is not a reference book, and there is nothing remotely systematic or comprehensive about which horses have been granted inclusion and which horses have not. The sole criterion is personal choice – no more, no less. Thus the pages that follow contain a good deal of material on horse racing but little about showjumping and nothing at all about polo or hunting. And you will have to go elsewhere for volumes about horse breeds, or horse-pulled carriages, or horse colours, or the evolution of the horse – fascinating as those subjects are.

Cross-references within the book are signalled with bold type and small capitals, thus: **ARKLE**.

Let Us Now Praise Famous Horses

I fell under the spell of horses early in life. From a very young age I was captivated by their appearance, their movement, their sound, their texture and their smell. Family lore insists that I have been devoted to horses since my first visit to a racecourse – the now defunct track at Lewes – when six months old. The first famous horse to engage my infant attention was Topper, the snow-white stallion who shared adventures with genial TV cowboy Hopalong Cassidy.

A series of happy chances in June 1957 brought me a place in the formal welcoming party when Hoppy – a.k.a. actor William Boyd – arrived at Waterloo station on a rare visit to England, having crossed the Atlantic by liner.

By my seven-year-old reckoning this afforded a golden opportunity for me to meet Topper, since the horse was bound to be accompanying Hoppy on his trip. I was frantic with excitement at the prospect of seeing the great horse in the flesh, but when the train arrived at Waterloo he was nowhere to be seen.

Baffled, I lingered outside the guards' van in case Topper made a belated appearance, but eventually I had to confront the awful conclusion. The horse had not been on the train.

I asked Hoppy whether he knew where Topper was, but he did not. Nor did any among his entourage. And as for the crest-fallen little boy in his brand new cowboy outfit (complete with gun), I convinced myself that Topper shared my disappointment. One day we would meet – but we never did.

When I was eleven, I started riding at the local stables, where I met the love of my life.

Dumpling was a barrel-like bay pony straight out of Thelwell, with four white socks and a large white blaze down her face – the same markings which years later would make Shergar so instantly recognisable. My beloved Dumpling did not possess Shergar's exceptional cruising speed, though she had enough competitive spirit to win us two runner-up rosettes in the Enfield Chace Pony Club Gymkhana in 1965.

Having outgrown Dumpling, I landed another runner-up rosette the following year on a black pony named Cinders – though to this day I am convinced that we would have won the Apple-Bobbing had a rival not bobbed my apple, rather than his own.

I graduated from ponies to full-size horses and struck up a good relationship with a hog-maned cob named Paddy, a horse with a keener sense of horsy humour than any I have encountered. When out on a ride, he would wait until my attention was elsewhere then drop a shoulder, and I would tumble out the side door. He never ran off, and I just got back into the saddle.

There was nothing malicious about The Cob (as he was known in the stables). Tipping me off was simply part of the game.

I cut my racing teeth on the hill at Alexandra Park, which offered the best free view in London. My father and I would mainly go to evening meetings at the course known as 'The Frying Pan' on account of its eccentric configuration, and once we had found a suitable vantage point Dad would scurry down through the hole in the fence to the betting ring, then nip back up the hill to where his son was working his way through Spam sandwiches and Tizer.

I started to experience the pleasure of following individual horses, and both in my imagination and on the racecourse, Arkle was in a category all of his own. For once, the word 'awesome' was inadequate.

I had watched him on television and had assiduously kept cuttings of his exploits since I first became aware of this steeplechasing phenomenon from Ireland. Seeing him in the flesh – just the once, in the King George VI Chase at Kempton Park in December 1965 – was unforgettable. Arkle was not classically beautiful, but he had around him a real aura, while on top of that arched head carriage sat the most remarkable pair of equine ears you would ever see. Long and expressive, they seemed to have a life of their own as they scanned the crowd, checking that everyone was looking at him.

More recently I have loved visiting the equine elderly, retired horses (often but not always former racehorses) turned out in a field, and – ideally – covered in mud.

It was in this happy condition that I discovered Flyingbolt (in handicapping terms almost the equal of Arkle) sharing a field with Cheltenham Gold Cup winner Fort Leney; dual Champion Hurdler winner Sea Pigeon; and many Grand National winners.

Arkle and Dumpling aside, my all-time favourite horse was Credo's Daughter, owned by actors James Bolam and Susan Jameson – and like Sam Kydd in a 1960s British film, not the star but still an indispensable member of the cast.

That ubiquity was part of her appeal. I never won serious money on her, and she never won a major race, but there was something hugely appealing about her: small and compact, always beautifully turned out by trainer Syd Woodman from his tiny yard in West Sussex, towards the finish of a race she would be plugging on when most of her rivals had thrown in the towel. In a wonderful sequence of five races in autumn 1975 she finished runner-up in the Mackeson Gold Cup, dead-heated for fourth place in the Hennessy Gold Cup, ran second in the Massey Ferguson Gold Cup and fourth in the SGB Chase – and then won at Kempton Park and was retired. As a broodmare she produced many good horses, notably the top-class hurdler King Credo.

Credo's Daughter and I lost touch in the years after her retirement from the track, but then I heard of her whereabouts – and a couple of phone calls later, I was with her in an Oxfordshire field. She was in her mid-twenties, dip-backed with age and distinctly rickety, but that brightness in her eye had not dimmed.

It was a one-sided conversation. She offered no special welcome, and try as I might, I could not persuade her to prick her ears for a photo. After a few minutes it was clear that my audience was over. She wandered off to graze with her chums, leaving me to mull over the old question: why is the relationship between horse and human so special?

In a way, the mare's indifference to me that day was part of her appeal. We think we can look into horses' minds, but we cannot.

As you may read in this book, in the section on La Marquesa, St Thomas Aquinas declared that you cannot love a horse because the horse cannot love you back. This is clearly a questionable view, as the horse might love you but not be letting on.

You might also reflect upon Simon Barnes's view in the piece on Quixall Crossett: 'Life: that is what horses are good at. That is what horses give.'

AARON
D.H. Lawrence's horse

Novelist D.H. Lawrence (1885–1930) was not renowned for his horsemanship, though there is a strong equine element in two of his best-known short stories: 'The Rocking-Horse Winner' (*see* **MALABAR**) and 'St Mawr'. A piece of DHL lore was that he was excessively fond of Aaron, and when the horse died, the writer had his hide made into a duffel bag.

AARVAK
In Norse mythology, the 'early waker'

One of the horses that draws the Sun's chariot, which was driven by the maiden Sol.

ACTAEON et al.
The horses of Helios

In classical mythology Helios – the Sun – has eight horses: Actaeon, Aethon, Amethea, Bronte, Erythreos, Lampos, Phlegon and Purocis. All snow-white, the horses of Helios climb up to heaven at the beginning of the day, then descend into the ocean in the evening.

The worlds of Greek and Roman myth teem with horses, only a few of whom resonate today. **PEGASUS**, for example, is worthy of his own entry later in this book.

Consider a few:

- Aurora, goddess of the dawn, has three horses: Abraxa, Eos and Phaethon;
- Pluto has four horses: Abaster, Abatos, Aeton and Nonios;
- One of Hercules's horses, Arion, was the offspring of Poseidon and Demeter, the mount of Adrastus, king of Argos;
- Balios belonged to Neptune (who also had Hippocampus) and later to Achilles;
- Cerus belonged to Adrastus;
- Cyllaros was one of the horses of Castor and Pollux, twin offspring of Jupiter and Leda – as was Harpagus;
- Dino ('the marvel') belonged to Diomedes, hero of the siege of Troy (not to be confused with the Diomedes who fed his horses on human flesh);
- Ethon ('fiery') was among the horses owned by Hector, as was Galathe;
- Phallus: the horse of Heraclius;
- Podarge: another of the horses of Hector;
- Xanthos belonged to Achilles.

ADONIS
George III's charger

The grey charger Adonis was the favourite horse of George III (1738–1820, reigned from 1760), and the best-known depiction of Adonis is Sir William Beechey's painting *George III reviewing the 10th Light Dragoons*. At the time of its painting, this portrait caused some ructions in royal circles.

In the 1790s George III was deep into one of his frequent arguments with his son George, later Prince Regent and then George IV, who was omitted from the original version of the painting. The story goes that when Queen Charlotte visited Beechey in his painting room at Windsor Castle, she remarked that her son George should have been included. Beechey suggested that including young George was more than his job was worth, but a compromise was reached by depicting the future George IV on a black horse, to emphasise the difference with the king on his white charger.

Shortly after the painting had been thus revised, George III paid a visit to Beechey, and did not like what he saw. 'Hey, what, what, what!' he is reported to have exclaimed. 'Beechey, the prince! D—n the prince!' The king demanded that the canvas be torn from its support and thrown out the window, but an equerry had the presence of mind to appropriate the discarded work of art, and in 1798 it was put on public display at the Royal Academy. Later it was displayed in the State Dining Room at Windsor Castle. Unfortunately its large size made it unwieldy, and it was destroyed in the Windsor Castle fire in 1992. A slightly smaller version is in the National Army Museum in London.

The distinguished equestrian author R.S. Summerhays

wrote that Adonis was 'sold in old age to perform in stage productions'.

AESOP

The horse and the donkey, and the horse and the stag

A donkey is heavily weighed down by his load, and asks for the horse's aid. The horse refuses. The donkey drops down dead. The horse has to carry not only his own burden, but the dead donkey's carcass as well. Moral: help your neighbour; if you don't, you may end up worse off.

Or try this one:

A horse and a stag share a field. The horse believes he owns the whole field, and enlists the assistance of a man to help drive the stag away. The man puts a saddle and bridle on the horse and moves the stag on, but is so impressed by the usefulness of the horse that he declines to restore his freedom.

Aesop's Fables – 358 of them – come in all shapes and sizes, and far from all are accepted as being invented by Aesop himself, of whom practically nothing is known, not even whether or not he lived. If pressed, some scholars opine that he was born in 630 BCE and died in 564.

One school of thought has him living as a slave on the island of Samos. Another places him in Ethiopia. Some sources assert that he was spectacularly ugly, but clever enough to endear himself to potential patrons.

Nor is there anything consistent about the fables themselves, many of which exist in several variations. For example, 'The Horse and the Donkey' can be 'The Ox and the Donkey' or 'The Donkey and the Mule'.

William Caxton, father of English printing, did not include

'The Horse and the Donkey' in his 1484 edition of *Aesop's Fables*, but did print 'How the Horse Lost Its Liberty' in the same edition, providing this moral: 'None ought to put himself in subjection for to avenge him on another.'

AETHENOTH
Lady Godiva's horse

The legend of Lady Godiva has existed in several different versions, but the basic story is common to them all. Leofric, Earl of Mercia and Lord of Coventry in the eleventh century, has been oppressing the people of Coventry with punitive taxation, much to the alarm of his wife Godiva. She pleads with her husband to reduce these taxes, and eventually he agrees to do so – on condition that she ride round the town on horseback and naked, to which she agrees.

Her flowing locks strategically positioned to spare her blushes and preserve her modesty – and the townspeople ordered to close their windows and not to steal a glance – Godiva performs her circuit of the town, and the earl keeps his side of the bargain.

There is a later sub-plot in which a young tailor named Tom steals a glance through his window and as a consequence is struck blind. Hence 'Peeping Tom'.

Sources for the Lady Godiva story tend not to name her horse (usually grey), but for those who like to take up the challenge of an unpronounceable word, in one source the horse is named as Aethenoth.

ALDANITI

'There is always hope, and all battles can be won'

Aldaniti, trained by Josh Gifford and ridden by Bob Champion, won the 1981 Grand National, and the 'back story' of the race made this running of the famous steeplechase an event dripping with emotion.

Less than two years earlier, at the age of thirty-one, Champion – one of the leading jump jockeys of his generation – had been diagnosed as having testicular cancer. His treatment for the disease was harrowing and lengthy, but throughout he was sustained by the assurance from the trainer that his job as Gifford's stable jockey was secure. And, in particular, Champion would continue his partnership with Aldaniti, a horse they had long considered well suited to the special demands of the Grand National.

But Aldaniti had himself been in the wars, having broken down – that is, succumbed to a rupture in a tendon – in November 1979. While Champion was restored to health, so was his National ride.

To general surprise, Aldaniti won his comeback race at Ascot, then started second favourite for the big one, preferred in the betting market only by Spartan Missile, ridden by fifty-four-year-old amateur jockey John Thorne. By the end of the first circuit Aldaniti had taken the lead, and he galloped on stoutly to win by four lengths from the favourite.

Aldaniti continued his racing career, and a year later he and Champion returned to Aintree for the Grand National. They fell at the first fence.

Champion retired from the saddle in 1982 and the following year founded the Bob Champion Cancer Trust, which has raised huge sums of money to support cancer research. His book *Champion's Story*, co-written with racing journalist Jonathan Powell, was a bestseller, and the movie *Champions* (1983) saw John Hurt in the jockey's role and Edward Woodward as Josh Gifford. It remains an inspirational and highly popular film, and a regular reminder of one of the greatest racing stories – well summed up in the rider's own words about the 1981 Grand National:

> I rode this race for all the patients in hospital. And all
> the people who look after them. My only wish is that my
> winning shows them that there is always hope, and all battles
> can be won.

Aldaniti died in March 1997.

ANMER
George V's horse in 'The Suffragette Derby'

As King George V's horse brought down by suffragette Emily Wilding Davison in the 1913 Derby, Anmer has earned a footnote in British history. The colt, named after a village in Norfolk on the Sandringham estate, started at 50/1 for the race, having won the Hastings Plate at Newmarket in April 1913 before finishing runner-up on the same course the following month. At Epsom, as the Derby field thundered down the hill towards Tattenham Corner, Anmer was running a race which justified his long odds, one of the stragglers in the fifteen-runner field and unable to respond to the urgings of jockey Herbert Jones.

Then Emily Davison darted out from under the rails, made a grab at the royal runner's bridle, was mown down and in a swirl of bouncing bodies the previously obscure Anmer became one of the most famous horses of all.

Emily Davison died in hospital four days after the race. Jones was not seriously injured, and was fit enough to ride Anmer – little the worse for his encounter with Davison at Epsom – in the Ascot Derby at the Royal Meeting two weeks later. They finished fifth.

Anmer ran four more times in 1913 and showed some decent form, though he failed to win another race as a three-year-old – and failed to reach a place in six outings in 1914.

In 1916 George V donated Anmer to the Department of Agriculture in Ontario, which was recruiting Thoroughbred stallions as part of a programme to improve the quality of local draught horses. Anmer enjoyed considerable success in his new calling, and was twice leading sire in Canada.

(There is a huge literature on the 1913 Derby, but for a comprehensive account of the plots and subplots of an extraordinary race you cannot do better than *The Suffragette Derby* by Michael Tanner, published in 2013.)

ANTARES
(and ALDEBARAN, ATAIR and RIGEL)
Chariot horses in Ben-Hur

First published in 1880, Lew Wallace's novel *Ben-Hur: A tale of the Christ* chronicles the life of Judah Ben-Hur, a highly bred Jewish youth accused by his former friend, the Roman Messala, of an attempt to assassinate the Roman governor of Judea – for which supposed crime he is sentenced to become a galley slave for life. But he escapes, finds his way back to

Antioch and enters the chariot race, where his five opponents include Messala himself.

Enter the quartet of Arabian horses, owned and bred by Sheikh Ilderim: Antares, Aldebaran, Atair and Rigel, described thus in the pre-race listing:

A four of Ilderim, sheikh of the desert. All bays; first race. Ben-Hur, a Jew, driver.

The chariot race itself forms the central episode of the novel, and Wallace does not hold back in his frenetic description of the climax:

Out flew the many-folded lash in his hand; over the backs of the startled steeds it writhed and hissed, and hissed and writhed again and again; and though it fell not, there were both sting and menace in its quick report; and as the man passed thus from quiet to resistless action, his face suffused, his eye gleaming, along the reins he seemed to flash his will; and instantly not one, but the four as one, answered with a leap that landed them alongside the Roman's car. Messala, on the perilous edge of the goal, heard, but dared not look to see what the awakening portended. From the people he received no sign. Above the noises of the race there was but one voice, and that was Ben-Hur's. In the old Aramaic, as the sheikh himself, he called to the Arabs:

On, Atair! On, Rigel! What, Antares! dost thou linger now?
Good horse – oho, Aldebaran! I hear them singing in the tents.
I hear the children singing and the women – singing of the
stars, of Atair, Antares, Rigel, Aldebaran, victory! – and the
song will never end. Well done! Home tomorrow, under the
black tent – home! On, Antares! The tribe is waiting for us,

and the master is waiting! 'Tis done! 'tis done! Ha, ha! We have
overthrown the proud. The hand that smote us is in the dust.
Ours the glory! Ha, ha! – steady! The work is done . . . !

In 1899 the novel was adapted into a stage melodrama by William
Young, and staged at the Broadway Theatre in New York in a
version noted for its lavish and spectacular production values.
The critic Walter Prichard Eaton described the production as
'a thing of bombastic rhetoric, inflated scenery, pasteboard
piety, and mechanical excitement', and it proved a huge success,
running for twenty-one years. It was estimated that over twenty-
one million people saw the play in New York.

Producer Arthur Collins brought a replica production to the
West End in April 1902, and this too proved highly popular. For
The Tatler's critic, 'The staging of such a play is just the thing that
Mr Arthur Collins revels in, for it requires all the ingenuity of a
master of stage mechanism to give the play the actuality of the
posters.' The critic representing the *Sketch* noted that 'the stage,
which has to bear 30 tons' weight of chariots and horses, besides
huge crowds, has had to be expressly strengthened and shored up.'

Naturally enough, particular interest focused on the
horses – real ones – and the stage machinery, which brought
an astonishing immediacy to the performance. The horses
galloped flat out towards the audience, secured by invisible
cables, and electric rubber rollers spun the chariot wheels. A
huge cyclorama created the sensation of dust and speed.

Ben-Hur was twice made into a film by MGM – a silent version
in 1925 and the epic 1959 treatment starring Charlton Heston
(who also starred in the 1961 movie *El Cid*: see **BAVIECA**) as the
eponymous hero, and it is in the latter incarnation that it is best
known today. The modern movie version has the lot: a huge

cast, mammoth set-pieces and four snow-white horses rather than the bays described in the book. And for connoisseurs of punting value, the film offers one of the best bets in the history of equestrian sport. Sheikh Ilderim is played by Hugh Griffith – who goes to Messala's camp to lay wagers for the big event and settles on odds of 4/1 against Ben-Hur. Those who availed themselves of such a wondrous price against the eponymous hero of the film were rewarded in the final reel.

ARCHER
Australian racehorse

Winner of the first two runnings of the Melbourne Cup, in 1861 and 1862, Archer was one of the most famous Australian racehorses of the nineteenth century. Trained by Etienne de Mestre, he was a five-year-old when landing the inaugural Melbourne Cup: carrying 9 stone 7 pounds, he won by six lengths. (The romantic story that he was walked the 500 miles to Melbourne from de Mestre's New South Wales farm – as connections could not afford the less arduous journey by boat – was demolished when in 1988 bills of lading were discovered which showed that Archer did in fact make the trip by sea.)

The following year he carried 10 stone 2 pounds, started 2/1 favourite, and won by ten lengths. In 1983 Archer was allotted 11 stone 4 pounds for the Melbourne Cup, but confirmation of his entry was not received in time – some suspected a stitch-up by the Victoria Turf Club in order to keep out the New South Wales-trained hero – and he did not run. Archer continued to race until 1866, when he was retired at the age of ten.

See also **MAKYBE DIVA**

ARKLE

The horse as national hero

Arkle – owned by Anne, Duchess of Westminster, trained near Dublin airport by Tom Dreaper, and ridden in all his steeplechases by Pat Taaffe – is widely regarded as the finest steeplechaser of all time, and with good reason.

He won the Cheltenham Gold Cup three times (1964, 1965 and 1966), Leopardstown Chase three times, Hennessy Gold Cup twice, Whitbread Gold Cup, King George VI Chase, Irish Grand National, Gallaher Gold Cup and many other big races – and his rivalry with his contemporary Mill House ('The Big Horse') made the 1960s a golden age of jump racing.

The true measure of Arkle's greatness is that the rules of handicapping had to be altered to accommodate his transcendence. From the 1964 Irish Grand National onwards, two handicaps were compiled: one to be used if Arkle was entered; another if he was not.

Just think of that. He was so good that he caused the rules of his sport to be revised.

In all, Arkle won twenty-seven of his thirty-five races, including twenty-two of his twenty-six steeplechases, and was renowned for his heroics when conceding huge amounts of weight to his rivals in handicaps.

But for all the big-race victories and the rolls of honour which he graced, what made Arkle unique was the effect he had on his public. The late Hugh McIlvanney, doyen of sports journalists, caught the essence of this when recalling the famous 1964 Cheltenham Gold Cup, when Arkle beat Mill House for the first time. McIlvanney wrote how, as Arkle began to close on the Big Horse, 'the incredible Irish support, the farmers and stable-boys and priests roared in unison: "Here he comes!" It was like a beleaguered army greeting the hero who brings relief. He came all right . . .'

Arkle was so adored that at the height of his racing career he was deluged with fan mail (much of it addressed to 'Arkle, Ireland'), and the deluge became a flood when that career was derailed by injury in 1966.

There were songs about him, poems about him, plays written around him, and when the slogan 'ARKLE FOR PRESIDENT' was daubed onto a Dublin wall during an election campaign, it seemed a perfectly plausible suggestion. And as with many an Irish hero, his daily feed was lubricated by regular bottles of Guinness.

He was put down at the age of thirteen in 1970 on account of a chronic arthritic condition, and his skeleton is now the prize exhibit in the museum at the Irish National Stud at Tully, County Kildare.

His memory lives in the Emma MacDermott bronze of Himself and Pat Taaffe in the centre of Ashbourne, close to the Dreaper yard, and the Doris Lindner sculpture at Cheltenham racecourse; in the happy bedlam of the Arkle Bar at that course; in the brisk trade in Arkle memorabilia; in Irish postage stamps; and in a readers' poll in the *Racing Post* which ranked Himself their favourite horse of all time.

Arkle is a true Irish folk hero, and as befits that role he has been recalled in song and drama. The rollicking ballad 'Arkle', written and recorded by Dominic Behan and issued as a single in 1965, describes the 1964 Cheltenham Gold Cup. Behan lampoons the stuck-up English racing men who sneer at the effrontery of the Irish-trained upstart taking on their champion Mill House – and are then left grubbing around for excuses after Arkle scoots up the hill and wins easily.

On the stage, Gold Cup day 1964 provides the background for Owen McCafferty's 2005 reworking of *Days of Wine and Roses*, the depiction of alcoholism best known from the 1962 movie.

The manner in which Arkle touched people's hearts has been widely chronicled, but nowhere more appropriately than in a leader column of the *Irish Times* the day after his death:

> That horse added to the lives of thousands. His instinct, which allowed him to put his power under human control – men are suffered by horses – had about it something that did honour to horses and to man.

(Ivor Herbert's biography *Arkle: The Story of a Champion* was first published in 1966 and issued in various editions since then. For an extensively illustrated account, see *Arkle* by Sean Magee – first published in 2005 and updated in 2009 and 2014.)

APOCALYPSE, FOUR HORSEMEN OF THE

See **FOUR HORSEMEN OF THE APOCALYPSE**

ARONDEL
Bevis of Hampton's warhorse

The horse Arondel (sometimes spelled *Arundel*) is a major player in the various Middle English verse romances which chronicle the eponymous Bevis in all manner of adventures.

While the depiction of a close bond between a knight and his horse is not uncommon in the literature of the thirteenth and fourteenth centuries (for example, see **GRINGOLET**), the bond between horse and master in this instance is unusually close. During his first battle on his new horse, Bevis praises his mount as a steed who fought with a loyal heart, and the affection and understanding is mutual – a bond which sees Bevis and Arondel victorious in the seven-mile race against King Edgar's knights, which Bevis enters with the intention of building the 'Castle of Arondel' from the winner's purse of a thousand pounds of gold.

Arondel and Bevis die on the same day, along with Bevis's wife Josian, and in a poignant passage the author of the romance describes how the knight finds his beloved horse dead in his stable. The final lines of the text chronicle how his son Guy, Bevis's heir, founded a house of religion where prayers will be sung for Bevis and Josian, and for Arondel, 'Yif men for eni hors bidde schel' – that is, 'If men may pray for a horse!'

ASTLEY'S EQUESTRIAN CIRCUS

Equine entertainment

Philip Astley (1742–1814) developed his facility for riding and breaking horses while serving in the 15th Light Dragoons during the Seven Years War. Discharged from the army in 1766, the following year he started working as a groom at a riding school in Islington, then a village near London. In April 1768 he opened his own riding school on Lambeth Marsh, where he soon became famous for his trick riding, his repertoire encompassing such feats as straddling two horses as they cantered round the ring and jumped obstacles, and performing a headstand on a pint pot perched on the saddle.

At sixpence for admission (one shilling for a seat), Astley's riding school was soon drawing huge crowds to witness the displays of equestrian daring. Astley's wife Patty did her bit, and later their son John was renowned for dancing on horseback. These displays were supplemented by clowns and acrobats to provide a varied entertainment closely related to the traditional circus we know today.

In 1769 the circus relocated to permanent headquarters – known as Astley's Amphitheatre – at the south-east side of Westminster Bridge, but performances were not confined to London. Provincial and touring versions of Astley's Equestrian Circus were staged all around Britain, while the Amphithéâtre Astley was founded in Paris in 1783 under the patronage of Marie Antoinette, and the Equestrian Theatre Royal in Dublin in 1788. Astley's horses achieved such fame that plays were written specifically for them. *Timour the Tartar*, for example, was described by one observer as 'contemptible' in literary terms, but 'the feats of the animals drew crowded houses, and the exhibition was the subject of surprise, as well as the object of delight'.

The essence of Astley's approach to his horses was gentleness, as avowed by the observations of the eminent veterinary surgeon Richard Lawrence:

> When the rider quarrels with his horse, he is generally the dupe of his passion, and the fray commonly ends to his disadvantage. Whenever you see a man beating any animal, it is at least ten to one that the man is in the wrong, and the animal in the right. A good-natured clever man may teach a horse anything, and it is a very mistaken notion that those horses which perform so many dexterous tricks at Astley's, and places of that description, are brought to execute them

by violent means. The fact is, they are taught by gentle means only, and by rewarding them at the moment they obey; hence they become accustomed by habit to combine the recollection of the reward with the performance of the trick, and it becomes a pleasure to them instead of a labour.

Lawrence described some of the horses' turns:

They would perform the figure of a minuet; lie down at the word of command; and, during a sham battle, fall as if dead, and not stir till they had permission. Gentle means, as already observed, were chiefly adopted for their instruction . . .

Astley's approach to breaking horses attracted the approval of George III, who in 1782 granted him a patent for his method.

Among the horses who found fame under Astley was the Gibraltar Charger, with whom he had been presented when discharged from the 15th Light Dragoons, and Billy, who supposedly lived to over forty and who was trained to count. According to one contemporary report, Billy 'would mark the name of Astley, letter by letter, in the earth; tell gold from silver and ladies from gentlemen; take a handkerchief from its owner; and "die" rather than fight for the Spaniard'.

On the outbreak of war with France, Astley re-enlisted with his regiment, serving as a horse-master in the Flanders campaign. The amphitheatre burned down in 1794, was rebuilt the following year, burned down again in 1803 and was promptly rebuilt again. In 1806 he built the Olympic Pavilion in Wych Street, off the Strand, as a smaller venue for plays and circuses.

In *The Old Curiosity Shop* (1841), Charles Dickens described a visit to Astley's:

Then the play itself! the horses which little Jacob believed from the first to be alive, and the ladies and gentlemen of whose reality he could be by no means persuaded, having never seen or heard anything at all like them – the firing, which made Barbara wink – the forlorn lady, who made her cry – the tyrant, who made her tremble – the man who sang the song with the lady's-maid and danced the chorus, who made her laugh – the pony who reared up on his hind legs when he saw the murderer, and wouldn't hear of walking on all fours again until he was taken into custody – the clown who ventured on such familiarities with the military man in boots – the lady who jumped over the nine-and-twenty ribbons and came down safe upon the horse's back – everything was delightful, splendid, and surprising. Little Jacob applauded till his hands were sore; Kit cried 'an-kor' at the end of everything, the three-act piece included; and Barbara's mother beat her umbrella on the floor, in her ecstasies, until it was nearly worn down to the gingham.

Philip Astley died in 1814, and the amphitheatre was eventually demolished in 1893.

ATAIR

See **ANTARES**

AUSTERLITZ

See **MARENGO**

BALAAM'S ASS

Talking equine in the Book of Numbers

In the Old Testament, chapter 22 of the Book of Numbers describes how Balaam, son of Beor at Pethor, is importuned by Balak, son of Zippor, king of Moab, to come and curse the Israelites, who are camped on the plains of Moab in such numbers that the Moab people are feeling distinctly threatened. God tells Balaam that he is not to curse the Israelites, for they are blessed. After Balaam is subjected to further importuning from the Moab princes, God relents and says – as related in the King James version – that 'the word which I shall say unto thee, that shall you do'. Now read on . . .

> So Balaam rose in the morning, and saddled his ass, and went with the princes of Moab.

But God's anger was kindled because he went; and the angel of the Lord took his stand in the way as his adversary. Now he was riding on the ass, and his two servants were with him.

And the ass saw the angel of the Lord standing in the road, with a drawn sword in his hand; and the ass turned aside out of the road; and went into a field; and Balaam struck the ass, to turn her into the road.

Then the angel of the Lord stood in a narrow path between the vineyards, with a wall on either side.

And when the ass saw the angel of the Lord, she pushed against the wall, and pressed Balaam's foot against the wall; so he struck her again.

Then the angel of the Lord went ahead, and stood in a narrow place, where there was no way to turn either to the right or the left.

When the ass saw the angel of the Lord, she lay down under Balaam, and Balaam's anger was kindled, and he struck the ass with his staff.

Then the Lord opened the mouth of the ass, and she said to Balaam: 'What have I done to you, that you have struck me these three times?'

And Balaam said to the ass, 'Because you have made sport of me. I wish I had a sword in my hand, for then I would kill you.'

And the ass said to Balaam, 'Am I not your ass, upon which you have ridden all your life long to this day? Was I ever accustomed to do so to you?' And he said, 'No.'

Then the Lord opened the eyes of Balaam, and he saw the angel of the Lord standing in the way, with his drawn sword in his hand; and he bowed his head, and fell on his face.

And the angel of the Lord said to him, 'Why have you struck your ass these three times? Behold, I have come forth to withstand you, because your way is perverse before me;

'And the ass saw me, and turned aside before me these three times. If she had not turned aside from me, surely just now I would have then slain you and let her live.'

Then Balaam said to the angel of the Lord, 'I have sinned, for I did not know that thou didst stand in the road against me. Now, therefore, if it is evil in thy sight, I will go back again.'

And the angel of the Lord said to Balaam, 'Go with the men; but only the word which I bid you, that shall you speak.' So Balaam went on with the princes of Balak.

(Numbers 22:21–35)

Suitably chastened, Balaam ends up heaping repeated blessings on the Israelites, thereby incurring the wrath of Balak: 'I called you to curse my enemies, and behold, you have blessed them these three times. Therefore now flee to your place.' The return trip seems to have been less eventful than the journey to Moab, with Balaam's ass keeping his own counsel and declining to comment – though he has a speaking role in the Chester Mystery Plays in the Middle Ages.

The Old Testament is peppered with references to horses, few of which are as powerful as the Book of Job, chapter 39:

Hast thou given the horse strength? Hast thou clothed his neck with thunder?

Canst thou make him afraid as a grasshopper? The glory of his nostrils is terrible.

He paweth in the valley, and rejoiceth in his strength; he goeth on to meet the armed men.

He mocketh at fear, and is not affrighted; neither turneth he back from the sword.

The quiver rattleth against him, the glittering spear and the shield.

He swalloweth the ground with fierceness and rage; neither believeth he that it is the sound of the trumpet.

He saith among the trumpets, Ha, ha; and he smelleth the battle afar off, the thunder of the captains, and the shouting . . .

BANKS'S HORSE

See **Morocco**

BARBARY ROAN

See **Capilet**

BARBIE
. . . in the Mongol Derby

The Mongol Derby is run over 1,000 kilometres (621 miles) across the Mongolian Steppes, broadly following the route established by Genghis Khan's postal delivery system, created in the thirteenth century.

The modern race was first staged in 2009, and claims to be the longest horse race in the world. The precise direction of the course changes from year to year and is only revealed close to the 'off', but whatever the route, the course always features a daunting terrain: mountain passes, wooded hills, river crossings and sandy dunes in addition to the steppes. And the vicissitudes of the weather add another layer of difficulty.

In order to negotiate this towering challenge, riders regularly switch to fresh mounts – those who complete the course will probably have partnered twenty-five to thirty different horses – and the equine natives tend to be less than fully broken. Sometimes they are downright unco-operative, all of which adds to the fun (which may not be quite the right word). Mounts are chosen at random, and riders tend to spend around fourteen hours a day in the saddle. This is emphatically not for the faint-hearted.

The course is punctuated by twenty-five horse stations, where veterinary checks are made.

The race takes at least ten days to complete (bring your own bedding), and if still undeterred, be aware that the entry fee is over £10,000.

Just getting round the course is a major achievement, but a special salute must go to 2013 winner Lara Prior-Palmer (niece of famed eventer Lucinda), who became the first female winner, and wrote up her experience in the book *Rough Magic*, published in 2019.

Prior-Palmer recalls a memorable mount, nicknamed on account of the blond colour of his mane: the diminutive Barbie. 'When I look at the photos now,' she reflects, 'I suppress my urge to ring the RSPCA.' In Mongolia, size, she declares, is not necessarily expected to dictate performance, and what Barbie lacked in height he made up with exceptional strength.

As well as becoming the first female to win this extraordinary race, Prior-Palmer established two other landmarks: first British winner, and, at nineteen years old, youngest winner.

BAVIECA
El Cid's horse

Bavieca – variant spelling *Babieca* – was the favourite horse of El Cid (c. 1030–1099), fabled hero of Castille in the eleventh century and today best known as the subject of the 1961 epic film starring Charlton Heston. At the climax of the movie El Cid's lifeless corpse is fixed astride his horse to encourage his troops in the belief that their leader is still fighting.

While El Cid – Rodrigo Díaz de Vivar – was a real historical character famed for his military achievements in conflicts with the Moors, through myth, legend and ballad he has been amplified into an ideal of knightly virtue. The French playwright Pierre Corneille wrote *Le Cid* in 1637, and the chronicles about El Cid were translated by the poet Robert Southey in 1808.

Southey relates how El Cid, when choosing a horse as a young man, passed over several fine-looking horses in favour of a particularly rough-looking colt, who was considered slow-witted. By way of response, El Cid called the horse by the Spanish word for 'simpleton': Bavieca.

The Chronicle of the Cid, published in 1808, has a poignant account of how Bavieca was cared for by the servant Gil Diaz after the death of El Cid:

> Gil Diaz took great delight in tending the horse Bavieca, so that there were few days in which he did not lead him to water, and bring him back with his own hand. And from the day in which the dead body of the Cid was taken off his back, never was man suffered to bestride that horse, but he was always led when they took him to water, and when they brought him back.

Gil Diaz bought two mares – 'the goodliest that could be found' – from which to breed from Bavieca and perpetuate his line, 'so that there were afterwards many good and precious horses of his race'.

The *Chronicle* describes Bavieca's death:

And this good horse lived two years and a half after the death of his master the Cid, and then he died also, having lived, according to the history, full forty years. And Gil Diaz buried him before the gate of the Monastery [San Pedro de Cardena], in the public place, on the right hand; and he planted two elms upon the grave, the one at his head and the other at his feet, and these elms grew and became great trees, and are yet to be seen before the gate of the Monastery. And Gil Diaz gave order that when he died they should bury him by that good horse Bavieca, whom he had loved so well.

BICHE
Byron's horse

Biche was the favourite horse of the poet George Gordon, Lord Byron (1788–1824).

In September 1816 Byron was on a tour of the Alps, and recounted his experiences in a journal he sent to his half-sister Augusta Leigh. On 26 September he wrote:

The greater part of this tour has been on horseback – on foot – and on mule; – the filly (which is one of two young horses I bought of the Baron de Vincy) carried me very well – she is young and as quiet as anything of her sex can be – very good-tempered – and perpetually neighing – when she wants any

thing – which is every five minutes – I have called her Biche
– because her manners are not unlike a little dog's – but she is
a very tame – pretty childish quadruped.

BILLIE
Hero of the 1923 FA Cup final at Wembley

When the Football Association arranged for the FA Cup final,
in those days by far the biggest single game in the football
year, to be played for the first time at the brand-new Empire
Stadium at Wembley in north-west London on 28 April
1923, the ground was believed to have a capacity of 127,000
spectators.

While the number who passed through the turnstiles to see
West Ham United against Bolton Wanderers was officially given
as 126,047, either the estimated capacity was considerably off
the mark or many thousands entered gratis, as a total of at least
200,000 people found their way in. Several thousand spilled off
the terraces onto the pitch, and the kick-off, scheduled for 3
p.m., was delayed as police struggled to clear the playing area
and restore order from the chaos.

Enter Billie (*Billy* in some accounts), a grey police horse
ridden by PC George Scorey, who would later tell the tale of
how he – and even more prominently his horse – wrote their
famous footnote in the history of British sport.

Before the game, Scorey – who was usually on duty on
Saturdays and claimed to have no interest in football – was
more concerned about Billie's behaviour than what would be
happening on the pitch, as the grey horse could be fractious. 'It
was the first time he really behaved himself,' reflected his rider.

That   afternoon, Scorey was part of a detachment of mounted police stationed a few miles from the stadium – 'I was thinking about my wedding and not about football' – when at 2.30, half an hour before the scheduled kick-off time, the command came for the mounted police to make their way to the Empire Stadium as soon as possible, as there was a problem of crowd control. Tens of thousands of spectators had encroached onto the pitch, and the mounted police were ordered to clear the pitch – 'Clear the pitch?' scoffed Scorey later, 'You couldn't see it!' – but now Billie came into his own, pushing firmly but quietly to move the overspill back off the pitch. Following the usual procedure, the police told the fans to link hands, and Scorey later said that his task was made easier by the unflappability of his horse and the precision with which Billie responded to instructions, and also by the good-natured respect with which Billie was regarded by the crowd.

It took around half an hour for the ground to be cleared and fit for the game to begin.

At the toss for ends, Hammers captain George Kay was heard to ask of the referee, 'What about the white horse on the penalty spot, ref?' But after West Ham had been defeated 2–0, their trainer Charlie Paynter had clearly been scoffing the sour grapes as he searched for excuses: 'It was a pitch made for us until folks tramped all over the place and that white horse thumped its big feet into the pitch.'

Billie's heroics were more appreciated in the House of Commons. When the chaotic cup final was raised during Home Office Questions on 30 April 1923, F.O. Roberts MP asked the Home Secretary whether he was 'aware of the almost universal praise of the conduct of the police, especially of the officer who was mounted on a white horse?'

George Scorey did not let his brief celebrity go to his head. After coming off duty at Wembley that evening, he went round to see his fiancée Kitty, who asked what sort of day he had had. He replied: 'Oh, just ordinary, lass, just ordinary.'

The approach road from the railway station to the new Wembley Stadium, opened in 2007, was named White Horse Bridge in honour of Billie.

(For dramatic photographs, see the official centenary history of the FA Cup by Tony Pawson, published in 1972.)

BILLY

See ASTLEY'S EQUESTRIAN CIRCUS

BINKY
Death's horse in the Terry Pratchett 'Discworld' novels

Watched by Mort, Death's new apprentice, the old manservant Albert is saddling up the grim reaper's horse when he reveals that animal's name: Binky. ('It just goes to show,' adds Albert: 'You never can tell.')

Mort recalls an image of Death's fire-snorting horse in his mother's almanac which he had devoured as a child – and never dreamt that this flame-breathing creature went under the name of Binky. Albert suggests the horse should have been called Fang or Sabre or Ebony – 'but the master will have his little fancies, you know.'

Although the Death of the Discworld describes himself as an anthropomorphic personification, 'he long ago gave up using the traditional skeletal horses, because of the bother of having to stop all the time to wire bits back on'.

The improbably named Binky is, therefore, a real, flesh-and-blood horse – which is not to say that he is an ordinary horse. He is much larger than average, extremely intelligent and extremely white: 'Not the off-white which was all that most horses could manage, but a translucent, ivory white tone.'

In addition to his superior stature and cleverness, Binky has learned a thing or two while carrying Death around the Discworld for hundreds of years, ushering souls into the next world. He can travel through time and different dimensions, and treats gravity as optional. Not only does he fly through the clouds to get Death to all the requisite shipwrecks, battles and assassinations, he also has a knack for walking not quite on the ground. Binky can tread on snow without leaving tracks – but has also been known to leave fiery hoofprints in the air when accelerating particularly hard.

He leads a comfortable existence in Death's stables, surrounded by gardens, apple trees and fields of corn – all black – and is well fed, judging from the quantities of dung that Mort is obliged to clear out on his first day in the job.

BLACK BEAUTY

Best-loved horse story in the English language

From the opening sentence – 'The first place that I can well remember was a large pleasant meadow with a pond of clear water in it' – *Black Beauty* weaves a beguiling spell.

Foaled on a farm, the handsome black horse with one white foot and a white star on his forehead is sold to Squire Gordon at Birtwick Park, where he encounters the other main equine figures in the book.

Merrylegs is 'a little fat grey pony, with a thick mane and tail, a very pretty head, and a pert little nose', while the suffering of the mare Ginger has touched successive generations of readers.

The original edition of the book, the title page of which reads *Black Beauty, his Grooms and Companions: The autobiography of a horse, translated from the original equine by Anna Sewell*, was published on 24 November 1877, by which time Anna Sewell was fifty-seven years old.

She had been born into a Quaker family in Yarmouth, Norfolk, and spent much of her life suffering from the after-effects of an accident at the age of around fifteen. She did not marry, living most of her life with her parents.

Sewell's disability made her uncommonly reliant on horses for mobility, and she became an accomplished horsewoman. In 1871, appalled and angered at the treatment of horses, she began writing her only book. With completion in sight she wrote to a friend:

> I have for six years been confined to the house and to my
> sofa, and have from time to time, as I was able, been writing
> what I think will turn out a little book, its special aim

being to induce kindness, sympathy, and an understanding treatment of horses.

When the book was finished Sewell's mother showed the text to the publisher Jarrold and Son (the company had previously published Mrs Sewell's Quaker tracts), and was offered a one-off fee of £40 (or £20 or £30, depending on your source) for the rights to the book. No royalties – just the flat fee.

Considering that the book is reputedly sixth in the list of all-time bestsellers in English, has reportedly sold over 40 million copies, and has been translated into countless languages, this was clearly a better deal for the publisher than for the author.

In commercial terms *Black Beauty* was a very slow starter, and sadly Anna Sewell did not live to witness its subsequent success. In April 1878, a mere five months after publication of the book which was to make her globally famous, Anna Sewell succumbed to lung disease, and was buried in the Quaker cemetery at Lamas, near the village of Buxton in Norfolk.

The ebbs and flows of Black Beauty's own fortunes – serving his time as carriage horse, 'job-horse' (that is, a horse for hire for single jobs), cab horse, etc. – are too familiar to need rehearsing here. But the book is much more than just an engaging story, and its backbone is the passion with which Sewell expresses her indignation over the treatment of horses – in particular the cruelty of the 'bearing rein', a device in the tack which connected the bit of a horse in harness with the pad at the top of the backband. In the mid-nineteenth century the bearing rein, designed as it was to force the horse into carrying his head high, proved the height of fashion among the carriage-driving gentry.

This fashion came at a cruel cost to the horse, forced to have his head literally reined in by the most uncomfortable and awkward means, and the rein was the specific form of cruelty to which Anna Sewell intended to draw attention.

The episode when Black Beauty and Ginger have been sold to the Earl of W— illustrates well the manner in which Sewell tackles the bearing rein issue, keeping the narrative going without preaching, but making her simmering anger clear.

The two horses are taken to the Earl's country seat Earlshall by John Manly, who hands the horses over to York, the coachman, to whom he gives a word of advice:

> 'I had better mention that we have never used the "bearing rein" with either of them; the black horse never had one on, and the dealer said it was the gag-bit that spoiled the other's temper.'
>
> 'Well,' said York, 'if they come here they must wear the bearing rein. I prefer a loose rein myself, and his lordship is always very reasonable about the horses; but my lady – that's another thing, she will have style; and if her carriage horses are not reined up tight, she wouldn't look at them. I always stand up against the gag-bit and shall do so, but it must be tight up when my lady rides!'
>
> 'I am sorry for it, very sorry,' said John . . .

Black Beauty relates the events of the following day:

> We heard the silk dress rustle, and the lady came down the steps, and in an imperious voice she said, 'York, you must put those horses' heads higher, they are not fit to be seen.'
>
> York got down and said very respectfully, 'I beg your

pardon, my lady, but these horses have not been reined up
for three years, and my lord said it would be safer to bring
them to it by degrees; but if your ladyship pleases, I can take
them up a little more.'

'Do so,' she said.

York came round to our heads and shortened the rein
himself, one hole, I think; every little makes a difference,
be it for better or worse, and that day we had a steep hill
to go up. Then I began to understand what I had heard of.
Of course I wanted to put my head forward and take the
carriage up with a will, as we had been used to do; but no, I
had to pull with my head up now, and that took all the spirit
out of me, and the strain came on my back and legs . . .

Day by day, hole by hole our bearings were shortened,
and instead of looking forward with pleasure to having my
harness on as I used to do, I began to dread it. Ginger too
seemed restless, though she said very little.

A trip to the Duchess of B—'s a few days later sees Lady W—
in demanding humour: 'Are you never going to get those
horses' heads up, York? Raise them at once, and let us have no
more of this humouring and nonsense.' But further tightening
of the rein is too much for the mare, who rears up, causes
mayhem, and is taken off carriage duties and given to Lord
W—'s younger son as a hunter – thus setting Ginger on the
slippery slope. Black Beauty is now joined in harness by Max,
whom he asks how he bears the rein:

'Well,' he said, 'I bear it because I must, but it is shortening
my life, and it will shorten yours too, if you have to stick to it.'

'Do you think', I said, 'that our masters know how bad it
is for us?'

'I can't say,' he replied, 'but the dealers and the horse doctors know it very well. I was at a dealer's once, who was training me and another horse to go as a pair; he was getting our head up, as he said, a little higher and a little higher every day. A gentleman who was there asked him why he did so; 'Because,' said he, 'people won't buy them unless we do. The London people always want their horses to carry their heads high; of course it is very bad for the horses, but then it is good for trade.'

The veterinary profession supported opposition to the bearing rein, and after the publication of *Black Beauty* the clamour for abolition gathered force. In 1883 five hundred horse doctors signed a petition against the device, and gradually fashion wilted in the face of popular opinion and the rein became less and less acceptable. And the book was given a sort of compliment when a pirated version was published by the American Humane Society in 1890.

But it took the RSPCA until 1914 finally to convince undertakers that they should not use the bearing rein for funeral horses.

Black Beauty has been adapted in all manner of ways, including several films, and its appeal remains undimmed – not least on account of its happy ending, which sees the horse restored to health after breaking his knees in a fall, and comfortably accommodated with a kindly family:

My ladies have promised that I shall never be sold, and so I have nothing to fear; and here my story ends. My troubles are all over, and I am at home; and often before I am quite awake, I fancy I am still in the orchard at Birtwick, standing with my old friends under the apple trees.

(The key source for anyone wishing to learn more about the extraordinary story of publication is Susan Chitty's *The Woman Who Wrote Black Beauty: A Life of Anna Sewell*, published in 1971. And for an enjoyable novel angle on this most familiar of books, see the chapter entitled 'Is Black Beauty gelded?' in John Sutherland's *Can Jane Eyre Be Happy?*, 1997.)

BLACK BESS
Dick Turpin's horse

. . . Or rather, not Dick Turpin's horse. Dick Turpin was a real historical character: Richard Turpin, the notorious highwayman born in Essex in 1705 and hanged on the Knavesmire at York (then as now the site of York racecourse) on 7 April 1739. After a life of brutal crime he had become the most wanted man in England, with a reward of £200 for his apprehension. But the identity of his horse as the faithful mare Black Bess is the invention of the nineteenth-century writer Harrison Ainsworth, whose novel *Rookwood*, first published in 1834, effectively solidified the modern myth of Dick Turpin the romantic adventurer (continued in such works as the 1974 film *Carry On Dick*). Ainsworth's admiration for the fictitious mare knows no bounds:

> Her sire was a desert Arab, renowned in his day, and brought to this country by a wealthy traveller; her dam was an English Racer, coal black as her child. Bess united all the fire and gentleness, the strength and hardihood, the abstinence and endurance of fatigue of the one, with the spirit, and extraordinary fleetness of the other . . . Is she not beautiful? Behold her paces! how gracefully she moves! She is off! – no

eagle on the wing could skim the air more swiftly. – Is she not magnificent? As to her temper, the lamb is not more gentle. A child might have guided her.

Bess comes centre stage in Ainsworth's novel on the famous ride from London to York, after Turpin has accidentally shot dead his confederate Tom King. Having evaded capture by the pursuing authorities, they come within sight of their destination – 'the towers and pinnacles of York' – when the brave Bess finally gives in to her exhaustion:

> Bess tottered – fell. – There was a dreadful gasp – a parting moan – a snort – her eye gazed, for an instant, upon her master, with a dying glare – then grew glassy, rayless, fixed – a shiver ran through her frame. – Her heart had burst.
>
> Dick's eyes were blinded, as with rain. His triumph, though achieved, was forgotten – his present safety unthought of. He stood weeping and swearing like one beside himself.
>
> 'And art thou gone, Bess!' cried he, in a despairing voice, lifting up his courser's head, and kissing her lips, covered with blood-flecked foam. 'Gone – gone! – and I have killed the best steed that was ever crossed!'

There are literary precedents before Ainsworth for Turpin having a black mare named Bess – notably an early nineteenth-century ballad which describes how 'Bold Turpin upon Hounslow Heath / His black mare Bess bestrode' – but to the author of *Rookwood* must be given the credit for inventing one of the great horses of literature. After Ainsworth, Dick Turpin could hardly be written about without Black Bess as his co-star, and she featured in numerous stage adaptations and other reworkings of the story. 'The Royal Hippodrome Performance of Turpin's Ride to York and the Death of Black Bess' makes an appearance in Thomas Hardy's *Far from the Madding Crowd*, first published in 1874, with Sergeant Troy playing Turpin.

Legend has it that the fictitious Black Bess is buried with the real Dick Turpin in the churchyard of St George's in York, and her ghost has been seen carrying Turpin in several locations – for example, up Trap's Hill in Essex (with poor Bess bearing the additional burden of the ghost of an old woman whom Turpin had murdered and is now clinging to her killer's back) and in Aspley Guise in Bedfordshire.

(For a highly readable modern study, see James Sharpe, *Dick Turpin: The Myth of the English Highwayman*, published in 2005.)

BLACK JACK
JFK's ceremonial charger

At the funeral of US President John Fitzgerald Kennedy on 25 November 1963, the formal procession was headed by a gun carriage pulled by six grey horses and bearing JFK's coffin.

Behind the gun carriage walked a solitary member of the Marine Corps bearing the presidential standard.

Then came a horse – a charger named Black Jack. Agitated and nervously prancing, Black Jack wore full ceremonial: bridle, saddle, saddlecloth with white edging – and in a particularly haunting image, riding boots reversed in the stirrup irons.

The fact that JFK had not been a cavalryman was beside the point, for the practice of involving a horse in the funeral rites of a great warrior has had a very long history – back to Genghis Khan and beyond. Underlying this dramatic practice was the belief that, although the warrior had fallen, he would be reunited with his horse in the afterlife. At its most extreme, the ancient ceremonials had the horse being slain and buried alongside his master; while this practice ceased long ago, it had been a tradition of state funerals in the USA that 'the caparisoned horse' would be at the centre of the proceedings.

The ceremonial horse was first included at the funerals of George Washington in 1799 and Abraham Lincoln in 1865, and since the Second World War has played its role in the obsequies of Franklin D. Roosevelt, Herbert Hoover, Lyndon Johnson and Ronald Reagan as well as JFK.

BLOSSOM and BOXER
In The Archers

See **MIDNIGHT**

BLUESKIN
One of George Washington's chargers

See **NELSON**

BOJACK HORSEMAN
Animated television series featuring alcoholic horse

Set mainly in Los Angeles, *BoJack Horseman* features the eponymous horse, a washed-up star of a 1990s series.

The first series began in August 2014 and the final programme was broadcast in January 2020, during which period the show

– which dealt with all sorts of uncomfortable subjects, among them racism and sexism – attracted a cult following.

BORDER FLIGHT
Samuel Beckett backs a loser

Playwright Samuel Beckett (1906–1989), best known as the author of *Waiting for Godot*, displayed no particular affection for horses, but had special reason to pay some attention to the 1964 Grand National. On 23 March 1964, while living (as he did for much of his adult life) in Paris, he wrote, in a letter to his friends Henri and Josette Hayden:

> Had a bet on a nag in the Grand National. It fell and the jockey broke his back. Five pounds down the drain.

That faller was Border Flight, who fell at the Chair fence (fifteenth obstacle in the famous Aintree race) and whose jockey was Paddy Farrell – who, as Beckett noted, broke his back.

But a dark cloud brought a silver lining as the terrible injury to Farrell, combined with the earlier career-ending fall of fellow jockey Tim Brookshaw, triggered the founding of the Injured Jockeys' Fund, the horse racing charity which has performed so magnificently over more than half a century.

BOXER
Carthorse in George Orwell's Animal Farm

Orwell's satire on communism, published in 1945, contains one of the most affectionately regarded horses – an enormous beast of nearly eighteen hands and phenomenal strength, who was not very intelligent but was widely regarded for his resilience and work ethic.

As conditions become increasingly worse for the animals under the repressive regime of the pigs, led by the despotic Napoleon, the loyal and unquestioning Boxer puts into practice his mantra 'I will work harder', rising ever earlier in the morning and working until – literally – he drops. On the orders of the pigs the sick Boxer is taken away in a horse-drawn van, and only Benjamin the donkey realises what is happening when he reads the words inscribed on the side of that van: "'Alfred Simmonds, Horse Slaughterer and Glue Boiler, Willingdon. Dealer in Hides and Bone-Meal. Kennels Supplied." Do you not understand what that means?' Benjamin screams at the other animals as the van moves out of the farmyard. 'They are taking Boxer to the knacker's!'

Then comes word that Boxer has died in hospital, upon which news Napoleon delivers an emotional oration, and declares that the pigs will be staging a memorial banquet to honour the horse. Napoleon winds up his oration with a reminder to the other animals that Boxer's regular maxims were 'I will work harder' and 'Comrade Napoleon is always right' – maxims, it is hardly necessary to add, which every animal should adopt as his own.

Benjamin the donkey, the oldest animal on the farm, never laughs and generally is of a cynical bent; for example, he points out that God had given him a tail to keep the flies off, but that he would sooner have had no tail and no flies. Apart from Boxer and Benjamin, the other named equids in *Animal Farm* are the motherly carthorse Clover, whose figure has not been restored since the birth of her fourth foal, and Mollie, the flighty white mare who draws Mr Jones's trap and who is inordinately proud of her ribbons. Mollie, predictably, cannot long withstand the privations of communal life at the farm, and defects to be cosseted by the humans.

An anonymous carthorse – the model for Boxer? – played a significant role in the creation of *Animal Farm*. While Orwell was thinking about writing an allegory of the Soviet system, one day he saw a small boy driving a gigantic horse along a narrow path, whipping the horse whenever he diverged from the intended route – a sight which made the author ponder that if such creatures as the carthorse were aware of their own strength, we should have no power over them. How men exploit animals was parallel with how the rich exploit the proletariat.

For all the sympathetic portrayal of the doggedly loyal Boxer, there is little evidence that Orwell was a great lover of horses. Certainly he took a jaundiced view of the preferential treatment of racehorses during the Second World War, writing in his journal in 1941: 'There are said to be still 2,000 racehorses in England, each of which will be eating 10–15 lbs of grain a day, i.e. these brutes are devouring *every day* the equivalent of the bread ration of a division of troops.'

BREE
Talking horse in The Chronicles of Narnia

The Chronicles of Narnia by C.S. Lewis (1898–1963) were published in seven volumes between 1950 and 1956. *The Horse and His Boy*, in which Bree (a Talking Horse who had been abducted by the Calormenes as a foal) has a prominent role, was first published in 1954.

The other horse who has a major part to play in *The Horse and His Boy* is Hwin, who had also been captured by the Calormenes as a foal.

BUCEPHALAS
Alexander the Great's horse

Bucephalas (frequently spelled *Bucephalus*) has an unequalled stature in equine annals as a real horse around whom has grown such an extensive web of legend that it is often difficult to distinguish fact from fiction.

The historical Bucephalas was of a Thessalian breed; was acquired by Alexander in 355 BCE, when the future conqueror of the world was just twelve years old; was high-mettled, tall, exceptionally well-proportioned, and coloured black, except for white facial marking; would have no rider except Alexander; was present at all his master's battles, including the occasion when he was stolen by the opposing forces, who returned the horse in the face of the direst threats from his master; died at the battle of the Hydaspes in 326 BCE – or possibly died of old age. Alexander led the funeral procession for the horse, and gave the name Bucephala to the city on the west bank of what is now the Jhelum river in Pakistan – though the site was severely damaged by floods, and the grave of Bucephalas cannot be located.

In the version of the story written by the Greek historian Plutarch, Bucephalas was originally intended as a mount for Alexander's father Philip of Macedon, and the horse's breeder Philoneicus the Thessalian brought him to Philip in the hope of making a deal. But Bucephalas behaved aggressively, rearing up and refusing to allow anyone to mount him. In the circumstances it was not surprising that Philip declined to buy the horse, and ordered Philoneicus to take him away – at which point young Alexander called out: 'What a horse they are losing, because, for lack of skill and courage, they cannot manage him!' Having seen what nobody else had seen, the boy took the reins and turned Bucephalas towards the sun. He had observed that the horse was frightened of his own shadow in front of him, and when his shadow was behind him, he calmed down.

Plutarch continues:

Then letting him go forward a little, still keeping the reins in his hand, and stroking him gently when he found him begin to grow eager and fiery, he let fall his upper garment softly, and with one nimble leap securely mounted him, and when he was seated, by little and little drew in the bridle, and curbed him without either striking or spurring him. Presently, when he found him free from all rebelliousness, and only impatient for the course, he let him go at full speed, inciting him now with a commanding voice, and urging him also with his heel. Philip and his friends looked on at first in silence and anxiety for the result, till seeing him turn at the end of his career, and come back rejoicing and triumphing for what he had performed, they all burst out into acclamations of applause; and his father, shedding tears, it is said, for joy, kissed him as he came down from his horse, and in his transport, said, 'O my son, look thee out a kingdom equal to and worthy of thyself, for Macedonia is too little for thee.'

Thus began one of the great man/horse combinations of military history, one which lasted until the death of the horse – and his death was an event which has divided historians, ancient and modern.

And why was the horse named Bucephalas, which means 'ox's head' in Greek? Did he look like an ox? Was the white blaze on his face shaped like an ox? Did he have horny growths on his head?

What is beyond doubt is that this horse has engendered all sorts of stories in romance and legend. In one, Alexander is passing by a cage when he hears roaring, which he takes to be coming from a lion – except that it turns out to be Bucephalas, who modulates the roar into an affectionate whinny, and gently raises his forelegs towards his master, in the manner of a submissive dog.

In another story, Alexander takes Bucephalas to the games at Olympia, where they compete in races, and where the horse increases their prospects by biting their opponents.

(Robin Lane Fox has written prolifically about Alexander the Great – and, by extension, about Bucephalas – including a biography, first published in 1973.)

BUCKBEAK
On Hippogriffs and Harry

The third book in the series about the boy wizard, *Harry Potter and the Prisoner of Azkaban*, was published in 1999. Among its many delights is the first appearance of Buckbeak.

Harry and chums (and Malfoy) are gathered in the forest to see Hagrid displaying the Magical Creatures, when Lavender Brown points to the opposite side of the paddock. There, trotting towards them, is a group of the weirdest creatures Harry has ever seen – half horse and half eagle. The equine contribution to their physique encompasses torso, hind legs and tail, while the aquiline side of the equation features talons measuring a foot and a half long, and steel-coloured beaks.

These are Hippogriffs, about whom Hagrid offers wise advice. They are easily offended. 'Don't never insult one, 'cause it might be the last thing yeh do.'

Hagrid selects a Hippogriff for Harry to ride, and it is on Buckbeak that Harry has his memorable maiden flight: once round the paddock, then back to the ground.

BURMESE
The Queen's favourite horse

Burmese was the black mare who carried HM the Queen for the Trooping the Colour ceremony every year between 1969 and 1986.

Foaled in Fort Walsh, Saskatchewan, in 1962, Burmese was given to the Queen by the Royal Canadian Mounted Police in 1969, when the RCMP performed at the Royal Windsor Horse Show.

At the Trooping the Colour ceremony in 1981 blank shots were fired at Burmese, and it is a tribute to both parties that they carried on as if nothing had happened. The Queen brought Burmese under control in an instant.

After the 1986 Trooping the Colour, Burmese was retired, spending the rest of her life at grass in Windsor Great Park, where she died in 1990.

But she is not forgotten, and residents of Regina, Saskatchewan, have a permanent memory of this unflappable mare in the bronze of horse and rider by sculptor Susan Veld in front of the Saskatchewan Legislative Building.

If Burmese was reportedly the Queen's favourite, many other horses have had a claim to her affections, and her passion for horse racing and breeding is very well known. Horses sporting the royal colours have won every English Classic race except the Derby: Two Thousand Guineas with Pall Mall (1958); One Thousand Guineas with Highclere (1974); Oaks with Carrozza (1957) and Dunfermline (1977); and St Leger with Dunfermline (1977). The closest she came to winning the Derby was in 1953 with Aureole, runner-up to Pinza three days after her coronation.

In addition to those victories in the English Classics, she has won many of the elite races, including the Prix de Diane (French equivalent of the Oaks – Highclere, 1974), King George VI and Queen Elizabeth Stakes (Aureole, 1954), Eclipse Stakes (Canisbay, 1965) and the Gold Cup at Royal Ascot (Estimate, 2013).

And her delight in all things equine is shared across her family. Her late husband Prince Philip, Duke of Edinburgh, was a leading carriage-driver; her daughter Princess Anne a major player in eventing (*see* **FUM**); and her son the Prince of Wales rode in steeplechases (though never rode a winner), co-owns racehorses with his wife the Duchess of Cornwall, and is an enthusiastic polo player – as are Prince Charles's sons, the Dukes of Cambridge and Sussex.

(There are many books about HM the Queen and her passion for horses – among them *Royal Racing* by Sean Smith, published 2001, and *Her Majesty's Pleasure* by Julian Muscat, 2012.)

BUTTERCUP
Racehorse celebrated by 'Beachcomber'

'Beachcomber' was the pseudonym of J.B. Morton (1893–1979), who for over half a century provided the regular humorous column 'By the Way' for readers of the *Daily Express*. The columns were populated by the likes of Big White Carstairs, Charlie Suet, Captain Foulenough, Mrs McGurgle, Mimsie Slopcorner, and Mr Justice Cocklecarrot, who is permanently involved in a law case involving twelve red-bearded dwarves.

Buttercup has been bought for £8 10s 3d by Dr Strabismus (Whom God Preserve) of Utrecht, who sets about training the horse for the Derby, insisting that the key to winning that famous race is to give the horse an inordinate amount of rest. Thus Buttercup spends two years grazing in a field and avoiding strenuous exercise, feeding on the doctor's specially prepared concoction of mashed arrowroot, wallflower seed, wet cement and celery.

But the revolutionary theories of Dr Strabismus (Whom God Preserve) of Utrecht prove less than effective. Buttercup does not win the Derby.

BUTTERMILK
Dale Evans's horse

See TRIGGER (1)

BYERLEY TURK, DARLEY ARABIAN and GODOLPHIN ARABIAN
Foundation sires of the Thoroughbred breed

It is a commonplace of equine history that the Thoroughbred breed had its beginnings in the import to England of three stallions – the Byerley Turk, the Darley Arabian and the Godolphin Arabian – at the turn of the eighteenth century. Every current racehorse is descended in the direct male line from one of those three. English breeders were looking to inject toughness, stamina and speed to complement their traditionally hardy bloodlines, and where better to look than the desert horses of Arabia?

The first of the trio to arrive was the dark brown Byerley Turk, foaled around 1680. He was probably a spoil of war, taken from the Ottoman army at Buda by Captain Robert Byerley, who then rode him at the Battle of the Boyne in 1690 before the horse took up stud duties at Goldsborough Hall in North Yorkshire. His modern descendants include Derby winners Blakeney (1969) and Dr Devious (1992).

The influence of the Darley Arabian on the breed – and hence on the history of horse racing – has been nothing short of sensational, with around 95 per cent of all Thoroughbreds tracing back to him, principally through his great-great-grandson **ECLIPSE**.

A bay horse born in 1700, the Darley Arabian was brought to England four years later after being sold to Thomas Darley, the English consul in Aleppo. In a letter to his brother, Darley described the horse as 'immediately striking owing to his handsome appearance and exceedingly elegant carriage'.

Darley sent the horse to the family seat, Aldby Park in

Yorkshire, where he remained for the rest of his life. He died in 1733.

The third founding stallion was the Godolphin Arabian, described as a 'gold-touched bay', who was foaled in 1724 and according to popular legend (which does not bear deep scrutiny) was discovered in Paris pulling a water cart. From France he was brought to Longford Hall in Derbyshire by Edward Coke, following whose death in 1733 he was relocated to the stud of the second Earl of Godolphin at Babraham, near Cambridge, where he remained until his death in 1753.

CALL TO ARMS
An unexpected slice of the action

At a stud the 'teaser' is a horse – often but not invariably sterile – who is employed to ascertain whether the mare due to be covered will be receptive to the attentions of the stallion booked to undertake the covering. The purpose of teasing is to avoid the risk of injury, inconvenience and wasted time should the mare not be ready. If the mare shows the right signs she will be put to the stallion, while the teaser meets and greets the next mare.

The teaser's role is a forlorn one, but there is some hope. In spring 1986 the Thoroughbred broodmare Branitska was about to be mated with the stallion Wolver Heights at the Stetchworth Park Stud in Newmarket. With horses, as with humans, the course of true love never did run smooth, and now there was a hitch. 'Branitska just would not take to Wolver Heights at all,' reported stud owner Bill Gredley, 'and kicked him like mad. In the end we brought the teaser forward, and because she stood still for him, we thought, "Why not?"'

The offspring of this unscheduled brief encounter between Branitska and the teaser named North Briton was well named as Call To Arms, and the colt posted some good form as a two-year-old, notably when beaten a neck in the prestigious Dewhurst Stakes at Newmarket in 1989, starting at 66/1.

As if the nature of his calling is not enough of a burden, the teaser has long engaged the attention of writers. In the *Racing Post*, Peter Thomas summed up the role: 'As far as I can make out, the teaser is the average-looking kind of chap who is forced to buy a lady several over-priced gin and limes at a night club before some open-shirted Adonis sweeps in from the sidelines to take her home.'

Not always, though – as North Briton would attest.

CANCARA
The horse in advertising

According to the report of his death in *The Times* in 2006, Cancara 'became a family favourite as he galloped across windswept beaches and clifftops during his sixteen-year advertising career for Britain's fifth-biggest bank, Lloyds TSB'. And the departed was also very good at rearing imperiously.

Cancara, who died at the ripe old age of thirty-one, was a black horse, but not any old black horse. He was *the* black horse, a familiar symbol of one of Britain's best-known companies. The scion of the Trakehner breed had been the Lloyds black horse since 1989, when he succeeded a horse named Beatos, like Cancara a professional to his fetlocks. 'You only had to show him a camera,' declared Beatos's handler, 'and he posed like a professional.'

Like many celebrities, Cancara had his own fan club, and did his bit for charity through personal appearances. He tirelessly raised funds for various causes, and it was a measure of Cancara's excellence for the Lloyds role that on retirement he was replaced not by just one other black horse, but by three: Dante, Tarantino and Imperator.

The practice of identifying a business through a logo dates back centuries, and the black horse, nowadays instantly recognisable for its association with Lloyds Bank, was initially connected with a goldsmith in Lombard Street in the City of London in 1677. By 1728 the image of the black horse was being used by another goldsmith, and it went through various guises before becoming deployed by Lloyds Bank in 1884. (Lloyds already had a beehive logo, and for a while the two designs jointly represented the company.)

It is not hard to understand the appeal of horses for advertising purposes, when the mix of power and gentleness, speed and malleability, control and freedom come together in an irresistible combination.

The 1999 Guinness advert featuring surfing white horses was voted top of a poll of the '100 Greatest TV Ads' in 2000, and more recently, Guinness again used horses in the advert which raised the question: 'Did I save the horse, or did the horse save me?'

CAPILET

Sir Andrew Aguecheek's horse

Sir Andrew Aguecheek is a mainstay of the comic subplot of *Twelfth Night*, one of Shakespeare's most enduringly popular comedies. Sir Toby Belch has manufactured a quarrel between Aguecheek and the servant Fabian – a confrontation the flaxen-haired coward would do anything to avoid. Report of Fabian's fencing skills prompts Aguecheek to offer: 'Let him let the matter slip, and I'll give him my horse, grey Capilet.' The mischievous Sir Toby mutters under this breath: 'Marry, I'll ride your horse as well as I ride you.' Those are the only mentions of the horse.

Other named horses in Shakespeare's plays include:

- **Dobbin** in *The Merchant of Venice*. Lancelet Gobbo, the clown, has been questioning his father Old Gobbo about his parentage: 'I am Lancelet, the Jew's man [i.e. Shylock], and I am sure Margery your wife is my mother.' Old Gobbo states: 'Her name is Margery, indeed. I'll be sworn, if thou be Lancelet, though art mine own flesh and blood. Lord worshipped might he be! What a beard thou hast got! Thou hast got more hair on thy chin than Dobbin my fill-horse has on his tail.' (A 'fill-horse' is a carthorse, 'fills' being the shafts of a cart.) To which Lancelet replies: 'It should seem, then, that Dobbin's tail grows backward. I am sure he had more hair of his tail than I have of my face when I last saw him.' 'Dobbin' is still one of the common names for a horse.

- **Barbary Roan** in *Richard II*. Not long before the end of the play, Richard, having been defeated by his rival Bolingbroke, is imprisoned in Pomfret Castle. The prisoner has a visitor:

KING RICHARD: What art thou? And how com'st thou
    hither
    Where no man ever comes but that sad dog
    That brings me food to make misfortune live?
GROOM: I was a poor groom of thy stable, King,
    When thou wert king; who, travelling towards York,
    With much ado, at length have gotten leave
    To look upon my sometimes royal master's face.
    O, how it yearned my heart when I beheld
    In London streets, that coronation-day,
    When Bolingbroke rode on Roan Barbary,
    That horse that thou so often hast bestrid,
    That horse that I so carefully have dressed!
KING RICHARD: Rode he on Barbary? Tell me, gentle
    friend,
    How went he under him?
GROOM: So proudly as if he disdained the ground.
KING RICHARD: So proud that Bolingbroke was on his
    back!
    That jade hath eat bread from my royal hand;
    This hand hath made him proud with clapping him.
    Would he not stumble? Would he not fall down,
    Since pride must have a fall, and break the neck
    Of that proud man that did usurp his back?
    Forgiveness, horse! Why do I rail on thee,
    Since thou, created to be awed by man,
    Wast born to bear? I was not made a horse;
    And yet I bear a burthen like an ass,
    Spurred, galled and tired by jouncing Bolingbroke.

- **Surrey** in *Richard III*. At Bosworth Field, the embattled Richard commands: 'Saddle White Surrey for the field tomorrow.' And not long after that, with Richard within seconds of defeat and death, comes the best-known horsy line in all Shakespeare – indeed, in world literature: 'A horse! A horse! My kingdom for a horse!'

Beyond those named horses, the Shakespeare canon includes set-pieces about the horse, such as the Dauphin's hymn of praise in *Henry V*:

> When I bestride him I soar, I am a hawk: he trots the air, the earth sings when he touches it, the basest horn of his hoof is more musical than the pipe of Hermes . . .
>
> It is a beast for Perseus: he is pure air and fire; and the dull elements of earth and water never appear in him, but only in patient stillness while his rider mounts him. He is indeed a horse, and all other jades you may call beasts.

An even loftier paean of praise to the horse comes in the poem *Venus and Adonis*, first published in 1593:

> *His ears up-pricked; his braided hanging mane*
> *Upon his compassed crest now stand on end;*
> *His nostrils drink the air, and forth again,*
> *As from a furnace, vapours doth he send:*
> *His eye, which scornfully glisters like fire,*
> *Shows his hot courage and his high desire.*
>
> *Sometime he trots, as if he told the steps,*
> *With gentle majesty and modest pride;*
> *Anon he rears upright, curvets and leaps,*

As who should say 'Lo, thus my strength is tried,
And this I do to captivate the eye
Of the fair breeder that is standing by.'

What recketh he his rider's angry stir,
His flattering 'Holla', or his 'Stand, I say'?
What cares he now for curb or pricking spur?
For rich caparisons or trapping gay?
He sees his love, and nothing else he sees,
For nothing else with his proud sight agrees.

Look, when a painter would surpass the life,
In limning out a well-proportioned steed,
His art with nature's workmanship at strife,
As if the dead the living should exceed;
So did this horse excel a common one
In shape, in courage, colour, pace and bone.

Round-hoofed, short-jointed, fetlocks shag and long,
Broad breast, full eye, small head and nostril wide,
High crest, short ears, straight legs and passing strong,
Thin mane, thick tail, broad buttock, tender hide:
Look, what a horse should have he did not lack,
Save a proud rider on so proud a back.

Sometime he scuds far off and there he stares;
Anon he starts at stirring of a feather;
To bid the wind a base he now prepares,
And whether he run or fly they know not whether;
For through his mane and tail the high wind sings,
Fanning the hairs, who wave like feathered wings.

CARTHORSE
Equine metaphor

'Carthorse' is not a name relating to any formal type of horse, let alone a breed; rather the description has applied to all horses whose lot in life is principally to move loads. The traditional image of the carthorse – a big, coarsely made and probably dim-witted animal – is of a creature who stands well down the equine pecking order and is readily exploited by man (see **BOXER**), but nevertheless he has enjoyed a decent career as a metaphor.

The most famous use of this toiler for metaphorical purposes is the carthorse's unlikely task of representing the London-based Trades Union Congress (TUC) in the work of the cartoonist David Low (1891–1963).

Born in New Zealand, Low had first drawn the parallel between organised labour and 'an honest but simple-minded draught horse' in his work for Australian newspapers before he moved to England to work for the *Evening Standard* in 1927. After the 1945 general election which returned Clement Attlee as prime minister, Low used the carthorse specifically to depict the TUC – to the understandable chagrin of the leaders of that organisation.

Low's carthorse never had a name, and when a newspaper competition was arranged to provide him with one, the cartoonist was less than impressed. 'The horse is a dear old thing,' he wrote in the *Standard* in April 1946, 'with a noble past and probably a glorious future. I refuse to give him a rude or inept name.'

Soon after Low moved to the *Daily Herald* in 1950, 'a dispute arose as to whether I was deriding draught horses or the TUC', which difference of opinion proved a contributory factor in his leaving that newspaper and moving to the *Manchester Guardian*.

The other equid which featured notably in David Low's work was the double-headed Coalition Ass, invented for mocking the United Kingdom's coalition government of 1918–1922.

CHIRON
Being a centaur

Labelled 'the most famous and wisest of all the centaurs' by one commentator, Chiron represented the acceptable face of centaur-dom. Offspring of Cronus in equine form and the Oceanid Philyra – hence his two-fold nature – Chiron was born an immortal, and was noted for his friendly attitude towards the human race. His many attributes included knowledge of music, ethics, martial arts and medicine.

All in all, a good-egg sort of a centaur – which is more than can be said for his fellows: they were the bad boys of classical myth.

Half man and half horse, the centaur is commonly human in front down to the waist; the torso and limbs are equine. In Greek myth, the centaurs were said to descend from Ixion, king of the Lapiths, and Dia, daughter of Eioneus, and lived mostly in the mountains of Thessaly and Arcadia. Their association with drunken and disorderly behaviour, which interpreters of myths came to characterise as the animal instincts getting the better of the more refined and cultured side of existence, was never better illustrated than in their behaviour at the wedding of Peirithous the Lapith to Deidiameia.

There were more guests at the wedding than Peirithous's palace could easily accommodate, and the Centaurs were among those who were moved to a tree-shaded cave nearby.

Unfamiliar with the smell and taste of wine, when they caught a whiff of its fragrance they brushed aside the sour milk which had been served up to them, and filled their horns from the wine-skins. In their ignorance they drank the wine neat rather than watered down, and soon were so enveloped in a fog of intoxication that when the bride entered their cavern, one Centaur leaped across to her and attempted to drag her away by the hair – and in an instant the other Centaurs were running amok among the women and boys.

In the ensuing ruckus Eurytion, minus ears and nose, was ejected from the cavern along with the other centaurs, who were then expelled from their home on Mount Pelion. They later fell foul of Hercules, engaged in his Fourth Labour, to capture alive the Erymanthian bull, and they make regular appearances in Greek myth as lawless and wild creatures, usually fighting drunkenly with only ripped-up trees for weapons.

For centuries the centaurs remained the incarnation of the tension between nature and culture. Their inclination towards lust, alcohol and violence stood as a counterpart to the value of civilisation, and their defeats at the hands of (for example) Hercules symbolise 'civilised' values winning the day over the baser instincts.

Since the time of the Greek myths there have been plenty of variations on the idea of the centaur, and not surprisingly these mythical creatures duly make their appearance in the world of Harry Potter: Bane, Ronan, Firenze and Magorian are centaurs who live in the Forbidden Forest, while **BUCKBEAK**

– a Hippogriff who shares some of the qualities of a centaur – takes the young wizard for a sky-ride in *Harry Potter and the Prisoner of Azkaban*.

CHAMPION (the Wonder Horse)
TV hero

All together now: 'Champion the Wonder Horse! Champion the Won-der Horse!'

Only twenty-six episodes of the children's television series *Champion the Wonder Horse* were made, but their popularity was immense. Created by television cowboy Gene Autry in celebration of his own horse Champion, the series began in the USA as *The Adventures of Champion* broadcast by CBS in 1955, and in Britain by the BBC the following year. It chronicles the adventures of Champion, a white-faced and white-legged chestnut stallion who in the wild in 1880s Texas has been indisputably leader of the pack. The horse has been domesticated to the point where he can be ridden – but never with saddle or bridle, and by only one human: young Ricky North, who lives on North Ranch with Uncle Sandy and Rebel, the German Shepherd dog.

For Champion, life is one hectic round of foiling criminals, disarming gun-toting villains, rescuing Ricky from shattered wooden bridges across ravines, alerting the locals to imminent natural disasters – you get the picture. Danger over and crisis resolved, each episode customarily ended with all the principal characters chortling merrily, unaware that another upheaval was only a week away.

Born in 1907, Gene Autry began his singing career on radio as 'Oklahoma's Yodelling Cowboy' before embarking on a movie career in which he made sixty-odd minor westerns. Having starred in *The Gene Autry Show* on US television between 1950 and 1955, he died in 1998 at the age of ninety-one.

CLEVER HANS
The horse who could count, read, etc.

The story of Clever Hans is comprehensively told in the essay 'The Elberfeld Horses' by Maurice Maeterlinck, published in 1914:

> Some twenty years ago there lived in Berlin an old misanthrope named Wilhelm Von Osten. He was a man with a small private income, a little eccentric in his ways and obsessed by one idea, the intelligence of animals. He began by undertaking the education of a horse that gave him no very definite results. But, in 1900, he became the owner of a Russian stallion who, under the name of Hans, to which was soon added the Homeric and well-earned prefix of Kluge, or Clever, was destined to upset all our notions of animal psychology and to raise questions that rank among the most unexpected and the most absorbing problems which man has yet encountered.
>
> Thanks to Von Osten, whose patience, contrary to what one might think, was in no wise angelic, but resembled rather a frenzied obstinacy, the horse made rapid and extraordinary progress. This progress is very aptly described by Professor E. Clarapède, of the University of Geneva, who says, in his excellent monograph on the Elberfeld horses:
>
>> After making him familiar with various common ideas, such as right, left, top, bottom and so on, his master began to teach

him arithmetic by the intuitive method. Hans was brought to a table on which were placed first one, then two, then several small skittles. Von Osten, kneeling beside Hans, uttered the corresponding numbers, at the same time making him strike as many blows with his hoof as there were skittles on the table. Before long, the skittles were replaced by figures written on a blackboard. The results were astonishing. The horse was capable not only of counting (that is to say, of striking as many blows as he was asked), but also of himself making real calculations, of solving little problems . . .

But Hans could do more than mere sums: he knew how to read; he was a musician, distinguishing between various harmonious and dissonant chords. He also had an extraordinary memory: he could tell the date of each day of the current week. In short, he got through all the tasks which an intelligent schoolboy of fourteen is able to perform.

The rumour of these curious experiments soon spread; and visitors flocked to the little stable-yard in which Von Osten kept his singular pupil at work. The newspapers took the matter up; and a fierce controversy broke forth between those who believed in the genuineness of the phenomenon and those who saw no more in it than a bare-faced fraud.

As Hans's fame increased, so did his repertoire. He would undertake mathematical calculations – including square roots – and spell out the names of people he knew; he would answer questions on a variety of topics; he would tell the time.

In 1904 a thirteen-strong commission (including a zoo director and a circus manager) was established by the Berlin Psychological Institute to investigate Hans, and could find nothing suspicious. Then psychologist Oskar Pfungst undertook a fresh, and more methodologically stringent, examination, publishing his results in 1907. Pfungst made several variations in the circumstances under which Hans was being asked questions. Von Osten would see the number before showing it to Hans, then show it to the horse without having seen it himself in advance; he would stand in front of Hans, and then behind; crucially, Pfungst established that Hans would give correct answers to questions asked by people other than Von Osten, which eliminated the possibility of fraud. Through conducting a wide range of experiments, Pfungst realised that Hans was picking up signals inadvertently given out by his master or other questioners. Hans, it turned out, was not so clever. He had worked out that if he responded to certain cues, he was rewarded with a sugar cube. As Stephen Budiansky wrote in his excellent book *The Nature of Horses*: 'Unconsciously, Von Osten was cueing Hans by tensing up as the horse started to count and then relaxing when he got to the right number.'

Clever Hans was, after all, just a horse, and far from the miracle he had once appeared. But he left a lasting legacy to the study of animal behaviour and psychology in general, for the subconscious response to the body language of another agent is known as the 'Clever Hans Effect'.

That legacy would have been little consolation to Wilhelm Von Osten. His objections to Pfungst's report fell on deaf ears, and he died a bitter man in June 1909 at the age of seventy-one.

COLE PORTER'S HIRELING HORSE
Great songwriter suffers life-changing injuries

Horses can be dangerous creatures, as Cole Porter discovered in autumn 1937.

Porter (1891–1964) had long been a giant of American popular music, having produced a steady stream of immortal songs such as 'Anything Goes', 'Night and Day', 'Just One of Those Things' and 'I've Got You Under My Skin'. Thanks to such songs, Porter's name had become a byword for wit and sophistication.

That autumn he was staying in Mill Neck, near Oyster Bay on Long Island, with his friend the Countess di Zoppola. The nearby Piping Rock Club hired out horses, and Porter proposed that the house party go for a ride.

An accomplished horseman, Porter loved the challenge of a skittish horse. 'If Cole were warned against a horse he chose to ride,' reported his friend Michael Pearman, 'it would be typical of him to spurn the advice and insist on riding the horse.'

There was just such a fizz-ball in the Piping Rock stable, and true to form, Porter was adamant that he would ride that horse. This turned out to be a catastrophic miscalculation.

Soon after setting off into the nearby woods, Porter's horse shied at a clump of bushes and ejected his rider from the saddle, then slammed down on top of him. Struggling to get up, the horse fell on top of Porter again.

Exact details of the accident differ depending on the source, but the upshot was that Porter suffered severe compound fractures in both legs. (Soon after regaining consciousness, he reputedly told the socialite Elsa Maxwell: 'It just goes to show that fifty million Frenchmen can't be wrong. They eat horses instead of riding them.')

Porter was subjected to a series of over thirty operations, and spent the rest of his life in severe pain. His right leg was amputated in 1958.

COLONIST II
Winston Churchill's favourite racehorse

In May 1951 Clementine Churchill wrote to her friend Ronald Tree about her husband's new enthusiasm:

> Have you seen about his horse Colonist II? He has won about ten races in a year and is now entered for the Gold Cup. I do think this is a queer new facet in Winston's variegated life. Before he bought the horse (I can't think why) he has hardly been on a racecourse in his life. I must say I don't find it madly amusing.

Despite what his wife wrote, Winston Churchill had a lifelong interest in horse racing. At Harrow School he celebrated a big-race triumph for his father's filly L'Abbesse De Jouarre. He rode in point-to-points and steeplechases at Sandhurst and Aldershot. In India he revived his father's racing colours so that he could wear them in pony races. And throughout his life he loved to attend race meetings and back horses. Clearly his wife's assertion that 'he has hardly been on a racecourse in his life' was wide of the mark.

In addition to his passion for racing, Churchill loved hunting. 'I do not think there is anything I would rather do than hunt,' he stated in his memoir *My Early Life*. And he was an enthusiastic polo player: at one stage of his parliamentary career he regularly played a few chukkas in the morning at Wembley before going to the House of Commons, of whose polo team he was a major player.

Horses are present throughout his life: from the pony Rob Roy, his first equine conveyance around the wondrous Blenheim Palace estate, to the racehorses he bred in the last years of his life. And horses had an important military role for him, notably in the charge at the Battle of Omdurman in 1898.

In *My Early Life* he recollected:

> Horses were the greatest of my pleasures at Sandhurst. I and the group in which I moved spent all our money on hiring horses from the very excellent local livery stables. We ran up bills on the strength of future commissions. We organised point-to-points and even a steeplechase in the park of a friendly grandee, and bucketted gaily about the countryside. And here I say to parents, and especially to wealthy parents, 'Don't give your son money. As far as you can afford it, give him horses.' No one ever came to grief – except honourable grief – through riding horses. No hour of life is lost that is spent in the saddle. Young men have often been ruined through owning horses, or through backing horses, but never through riding them; unless of course they break their necks, which, taken at a gallop, is a very good death to die.

If Winston Churchill was devoted to matters equestrian all his life, his passion reached a new level through the iron-grey French-bred horse who arrived at the Epsom stables of trainer Walter Nightingall in 1949; the horse that, according to Churchill's friend Lord Camrose, 'Providence brought him for his old age'. That horse was Colonist II.

Between 1949 and 1951, Colonist ran twenty-three times in the 'pink, chocolate sleeves and cap' colours which his owner had registered. His thirteen victories featured six in a row in 1950, and the individual prizes he won included high-quality races at Ascot, Goodwood, Sandown Park, Kempton Park, Newmarket and the now defunct Hurst Park (near Hampton

Court). His three wins at Hurst Park included, appropriately enough, the Winston Churchill Stakes – named in his honour – in 1951.

That day Churchill was entertained to lunch in the Hurst Park royal box by Princess Elizabeth, whose father George VI had Above Board running in the Churchill race. After Colonist had beaten the royal runner, Churchill received a congratulatory telegram from the king, and a few days later he wrote to Princess Elizabeth:

> I must thank Your Royal Highness for so kindly asking me
> to luncheon with you at Hurst Park last Saturday, and for
> the gracious congratulations with which you honoured me.
> I wish indeed that we both could have been victorious – but
> that would have been no foundation for the excitements and
> liveliness of the Turf.

Colonist II went on to greater things in 1951 – at least in terms of the form book – by finishing runner-up in the Gold Cup at Royal Ascot and fourth in the inaugural King George VI and Queen Elizabeth Stakes on the same course.

For *Racehorses of 1951*, Colonist was 'one of the most consistent, game and tenacious battlers seen on English racecourses this century: at his best when striding along in front and setting the others with the job of catching him and making them battle it out to the last: if not quite a champion in merit, in fighting qualities he was a great horse'.

Such a reputation made Colonist a good prospect as a stallion, but Nightingall's suggestion to his owner – by then prime minister again – that he keep ownership when the grey was at stud provoked the famous retort:

To stud? And have it said that the Prime Minister of Great
Britain is living on the immoral earnings of a horse?

Soon after Colonist II had started his new, reproductive
career, Churchill was asked by a friend whether Colonist was
still racing. Churchill's reply was: 'No, he has given up racing.
He is now rogering.'

An indication of Churchill's commitment to racing is the
fact that in old age he not only owned racehorses, he bred
them as well. Two of the colts delivered at his Newchapel Stud,
near his country house Chartwell, in 1957 were to prove top-
class performers. Vienna won six races and finished third in
the 1960 St Leger, while High Hat won four times – including
the Winston Churchill Stakes in 1961.

Among other Churchill racehorses worthy of note are
Dark Issue (won the Irish One Thousand Guineas in 1955);
Welsh Abbot (Portland Handicap at Doncaster, 1958); Tudor
Monarch (Stewards' Cup at Goodwood, 1950); Le Pretendant,
who had shown such a high level of form that he was invited
to the Washington International in 1956; and the top-class
hurdler Sun Hat.

Churchill's daughter Mary, whose husband Christopher
Soames had been instrumental in arranging and encouraging
her father's racing and breeding interests, wrote that the sport
had given Churchill 'enormous pleasure and interest in his old age'.

That pleasure was most purely distilled in Colonist II, the
grey horse with the never-say-die attitude, whose memory
Churchill kept alive. He commissioned Raoul Millais to paint
a portrait of the horse, which he declared 'a masterpiece –
charming in every way' and which now hangs at Chartwell.

Another portrait of the horse hangs in Churchill's bedroom,

which features paintings of his mother and his father, and on the bedside table is a framed horseshoe containing a photograph of Colonist II.

And Winston Churchill's racing colours are perpetuated in the scarf of Churchill College, Cambridge, founded in 1960 as a permanent memorial and home of the Churchill Archives.

(For more information, see *Churchill at the Gallop* by Brough Scott, published in 2018.)

CONRAD
First faller at Becher's Brook

Becher's Brook, the world's most famous steeplechase obstacle, is the sixth fence jumped on the first circuit of the Grand National at Aintree, and the twenty-second fence on the second circuit. It takes its name from Captain Martin Becher, who in the 1839 Grand Liverpool Steeplechase – the race which became the Grand National – was riding a horse named Conrad across an obstacle described as 'a strong paling, next a rough, high jagged hedge, and lastly a brook about six feet wide'. Conrad hit the 'paling' hard and deposited his rider in the brook, from where he reportedly surfaced with the declaration, 'Water is no damned use without brandy!' and remounted Conrad. The partnership was only reunited temporarily, however, as Becher found himself deposited in the water again at the next brook, now known as Valentine's. The modern Becher's Brook consists of a fence 4ft 6in high on the take-off side but with a drop on the landing side.

'Becher's Brook' has entered the wider language as an expression of a significant obstacle to be overcome.

(See *Aintree* by John Pinfold, 2017.)

COPENHAGEN
Duke of Wellington's charger at Waterloo

Scarcely bigger than a pony but endowed with limitless stamina and resolution, Copenhagen was foaled in 1808. He won two of the twelve races in which he ran, and was then sold to Sir Charles Vane (later the Marquess of Londonderry) before embarking on a military career.

Arthur Wellesley (1769–1852), who became the first Duke of Wellington, acquired Copenhagen and rode him in several battles, notably Waterloo, when he rode the horse for the entire seventeen-hour conflict.

The story goes that at the end of the day, with the battle won, Wellington dismounted from Copenhagen and slapped him gratefully on his flank – at which the horse lashed out with his hind legs and narrowly missed his master's head.

The equine war hero was retired from service and spent the rest of his days at the Wellington country home, Stratfield Saye in Hampshire, where he lived in the lap of luxury, reportedly devouring bath buns, chocolate creams and sponge, and, according to one source, 'ate his apples with all possible grace'. His laid-back demeanour allowed him to take small children for rides around the estate, and among his eccentricities was to eat only when lying down.

Copenhagen died at the venerable equine age of twenty-eight in February 1836, and was buried in his paddock. *The Times* reported:

> By the orders of His Grace, a salute was fired over his grave, and thus he was buried as he had lived with full military honours.

Later a memorial stone was erected, with this inscription:

Here lies COPENHAGEN
the charger ridden by the Duke of Wellington
the entire day at the Battle of Waterloo.
Born 1808, died 1836.
God's humbler instrument, though meaner clay,
Should share the glory of that glorious day.

And the Duke of Wellington himself paid his own tribute:

There have been many faster horses, no doubt some handsomer, but for bottom and endurance I never saw his fellow.

Copenhagen (played by Daniel Rigby) corresponds with Napoleon's horse **MARENGO** (played by Stephen Fry) in the BBC radio comedy series *Warhorses of Letters*.

CWRW

Name that horse

Cwrw, winner of the Two Thousand Guineas at Newmarket in 1812, is the only winner of an English Classic whose name contained no vowels.

If pronunciation of that name looks like a significant challenge, try pronouncing three vowel-free horses from the Arthurian tale *Culhwch and Olwen*, written in Wales in the early twelfth century: Hwyrdyddwg, Drwgdyddwg and Llwyrdyddwg.

Names are a source of endless fun in the horse world, and have been for centuries. The historian Keith Thomas, in his fascinating book *Man and the Natural World*, pointed out that giving a domestic animal a personal name made it special, and distinguished it from all other creatures.

The fascination with naming is widespread throughout horse racing (where in 1998 a sire named Pursuit Of Love impregnated a mare named My Discovery, and the resulting foal was named Geespot) and in other areas of equestrian business.

For instance, Don Quixote is very vexed about the name which he will give to his horse, and finds that ROCINANTE fits the bill: see page 182.

Indeed, many more of the horses featured in these pages have noteworthy names, while other horse names are more downbeat, some inextricably so: Sid, Eric and The Pub, and the gloriously dismal Keith's Fridge, to name but a few.

Then there are the naughty ones, like Who Gives A Donald, who ran in 1989; or Wear The Fox Hat, a two-year-old filly entered in a race at Folkestone in 1995. The authorities were uncomfortable with the name and requested an alternative, and the outcome was that Wear The Fox Hat became Nameless.

For more horse names, and then some, see *Fifty Shades of Hay* by David Ashforth, published in 2018. And while on the theme of hay, consider the case of the racehorse named Hay Chewed. (Think Beatles.)

CYCLOPED

Horse power on trial

In October 1829 the Rainhill Trials in what was then Lancashire were arranged between various inventors and engineers to find a new means of locomotion, to run on rails.

Five devices were to be tried out over one mile at Rainhill, including the 'Cycloped' – the invention of Thomas Shaw Brandreth of Liverpool. *Mechanics Magazine* described the principle behind the machine's construction:

> The motive power in this engine is gained in the same way as in the tread-mills of prison celebrity, and the dog-mills which we have sometimes heard of – only that horses, instead of men or dogs, are the agents employed. A still nearer resemblance to it may be traced in the common squirrel-cage, if the reader will, but for the sake of the comparison, suppose that the squirrel drives its circular cage round by treading on the outside instead of the inside.
>
> A common waggon-frame mounted on wheels is divided longitudinally into two compartments or stalls, and the bottom of each of these stalls is occupied by an endless chain of crossbars, which work into and revolve round the axles of the carriage. The horses are placed in the stalls, and by treading on the endless chains produce the rotary motion to propel themselves and the carriage forward.

In short, the Cycloped simply worked on the principle of the treadmill, and this was not enough to produce speed of more than four miles an hour, well short of what was required.

On the second day of the trials the Cycloped was the first of the quintet to be eliminated, its exclusion inevitable after one of the horses fell through the floor – though according to *The Times*, he 'was extricated without much injury'.

The competition was won by Robert Stephenson, who had maintained an average speed for the mile of 13.8 miles per hour.

CYRIL PROUDBOTTOM
In the Disney treatment of The Wind in the Willows

The horse Cyril Proudbottom is one of the main characters in the Walt Disney short films *The Adventures of Ichabod and Mr Toad* and *Mickey's Christmas Carol*, both released in 1949. He makes a cameo appearance in *Who Framed Roger Rabbit?* but does not appear in the original novels *The Wind in the Willows* or *Toad of Toad Hall.*

DANDRUFF

A racing certainty for Nigel Molesworth

Whizz For Atomms, by author Geoffrey Willans and illustrator Ronald Searle, is the third of the four books which make up *The Compleet Molesworth*, that hilarious chronicle of the world of a prep-school boy published in 1956.

Having declared that – in Nigel Molesworth's highly eccentric spelling – 'every boy ort to equip himself for life by knoing a bit about horse racing', Nigel turns his attention to which horse will win the 3.30 at Sponger's Park. Favourite at odds of 51/1 on is Dandruff, who has been selected by tipsters 'Preposterous' of the *Daily Plug*, 'Mendax' of *The Smugg*, 'On the Ball' of the *Daily Shame* and 'Alcestes' of *Farmer's Joy*. Molesworth is quickly convinced that everything is in Dandruff's favour. He has won over the distance; has two ancestors from the National Stud;

has a French owner; is trained on meat; sits up in his stable; is ridden by Lester Piggott; has firm going – 'THE LOT'. With all the boxes ticked, it is time, in Nigel's rallying cry, to 'BASH ON THE WINE GUMS'.

Dandruff seems a racing certainty, but finishes unplaced behind Bees Knees, Clot and Morbid. Molesworth drowns his sorrows in Pepsi Cola, before attending the racecourse, where he has a memorable encounter with the weedy Fotherington-Tomas, who proclaims: 'Hurrah hurrah how good it is to be alive and the horse is the frend of man!' – at which point a beer bottle thrown from a passing coach falls on his head, and he is borne away.

The racing section of *The Compleet Molesworth* ends with the admonition that boys should keep away from racecourses, as the sport is crooked. Open the newspaper and see how grim the world situation has become – and what catches your eye: '4.00 . . . Coarse Wire . . . Nankie-Poo can't miss.'

BASH ON THE WINE GUMS!

DAPPLE
Sancho Panza's ass

See ROCINANTE

DARKIE
Equine heart-throb

Darkie is Ross Poldark's horse in the *Poldark* novels. In the television version which commenced in 2015, the role was played by a black horse named Seamus, who proved so popular that he soon had his own Facebook page.

DARLEY ARABIAN
Co-founder of the Thoroughbred breed

See **BYERLEY TURK**

DELILAH
The Steptoes' horse

See **HERCULES**

DEMOCRAT
Top-class racehorse – then Lord Kitchener's charger

Democrat, a chestnut with four white socks, was rated the best two-year-old of 1899 after winning seven races, including the Coventry Stakes at Royal Ascot, in which he beat subsequent Triple Crown winner Diamond Jubilee; the prestigious National Breeders' Produce Stakes at Sandown Park; Champagne Stakes at Doncaster; and the Middle Park Plate (now Middle Park Stakes) and Dewhurst Stakes at Newmarket.

On the strength of such a record Democrat became winter favourite for the 1900 Derby, but in that race he could only finish down the field behind Diamond Jubilee – a horse he had beaten three times as a two-year-old. In autumn 1900 Democrat was put through the sale ring, and found a new home, joining trainer Richard Marsh for a mere 290 guineas. Marsh clearly liked his new acquisition – 'A quieter and better mannered animal you could not have wished for' – but he never recovered the form of his younger days.

What qualifies Democrat for a place in this book is his remarkable second career.

In summer 1902 Richard Marsh met Lord Kitchener, who was about to depart for India to serve as Commander-in-Chief of the army, and who asked the trainer if he could find him a Thoroughbred who would make a good ceremonial charger. Marsh suggested Democrat, who clearly made the right impression on the famous soldier, who wrote to Marsh after Democrat had completed the journey from England: 'Democrat arrived right and is a charming horse. I think he will suit me admirably.'

Democrat did just that, remaining in India for six years, during which time he carried Kitchener in his ceremonial duties, and as a sideline won prizes in show classes at local equestrian events.

(Democrat was ridden in several races by the Indiana-born jockey James Forman Sloan – named 'Tod' by his father on account of his diminutive stature. Sloan introduced the style of riding with very short stirrup leathers – he was derided as a 'monkey on a stick', but the style was highly effective – and was a brilliant tactician, in particular with the pioneer tactic of taking the lead and 'waiting in front'. To 'do a Tod Sloan' became rhyming slang for going out on your own: hence 'on your Tod'.)

DESERT ORCHID
National treasure

A measure of just how far Desert Orchid had become a national institution came in March 1991 when Norman Lamont, then Chancellor of the Exchequer, stood up in the House of Commons to deliver his budget speech.

Not long previously, an opinion poll had indicated that

while 84 per cent of people had heard of Desert Orchid, only 77 per cent had heard of Lamont.

Aware of the political capital to be gained from associating himself with a celebrity, Lamont declared: 'Desert Orchid and I have a lot in common. We are both greys, vast sums of money are riding on our performance, the opposition hopes we will fall at the first fence, and we are both carrying too much weight.'

How we chuckled!

And further evidence of the affection he generated came when, despite his not having raced for many years, his death in November 2006 was front-page news. 'He captured the nation's imagination as no horse has done before or since,' wrote *The Times*.

Devotees of **ARKLE** might dispute that claim, but there is no doubting the depth of the public's love of the steeplechaser widely known as 'Dessie', and the reasons for that love are not hard to pin down.

For a start, there was his sheer physical presence: a headstrong grey horse with apparently limitless reserves of power and sheer enthusiasm. Then there was his style of racing: a relentless gallop designed to grind his rivals into submission, and a flamboyant, exhilarating, attacking attitude towards the fences. To witness Desert Orchid at full throttle was one of the great sights of sport.

His racing record was highly impressive. He ran in seventy-two races and won thirty-four of them, including such prestigious contests as the King George VI Chase at Kempton Park four times (1986, 1988, 1989 and 1990), Irish Grand National, Whitbread Gold Cup, Racing Post Chase and Tingle Creek Chase.

But the single Dessie race which will live in sport's collective memory is the 1989 Cheltenham Gold Cup. Heavy rain and snow had made the going so bad that there had been a serious possibility of abandonment; worse, Dessie appeared to dislike Cheltenham. Everything was against him, but when the race shook down to a war of attrition with outsider Yahoo up the final hill, he found new supplies of determination. Cue the legendary BBC commentator Peter O'Sullevan:

> It's Desert Orchid on the near side, Yahoo on the far side
> – Desert Orchid drifting over towards the stands side. He's
> beginning to get up! Desert Orchid is beginning to get up as
> they race towards the line! There's a tremendous cheer from
> the crowd, as Dessie is going to win it! Desert Orchid has
> won the Gold Cup, Yahoo is second, third is Charter Party . . .

The memory of Desert Orchid persists. Readers of the *Racing Post* voted the 1989 Gold Cup as the greatest of the great races, and a life-sized bronze of the grey overlooks the Kempton Park paddock. As yet, Norman Lamont has no similar memorial.

(The compelling inside story of Desert Orchid's career is told by his co-owner Richard Burridge in *The Grey Horse*, published in 1992.)

DEVON LOCH
Racing's most famous loser

Queen Elizabeth the Queen Mother, who died in 2002 at the age of 101, was a passionate supporter of National Hunt racing, and owned over four hundred winners. But the race with which she will be remembered for ever resulted in the most sensational defeat of all.

In 1956 her steeplechaser Devon Loch started 100/7 co-fourth favourite for the Grand National, and as the race entered its closing stages he and jockey Dick Francis had seen off all his rivals with a virtuoso display of jumping.

At the last fence he was clear of his nearest pursuer ESB and still full of running. Past the 'Elbow' – the dog-leg stretch of the course which takes the runners to the winning post – he was galloping home strongly, when with fifty yards to go he seemed to jump a phantom obstacle, leapt into the air, belly-flopped and slithered to a halt.

Dick Francis had a unique vantage point from which to witness an extraordinary moment, and wrote in his autobiography: 'He fell flat on his belly, his limbs splayed out sideways and backwards in unnatural angles, and when he stood up he could hardly move.'

The Queen Mother showed remarkable stoicism in her reaction to a shattering blow. It was reported that in the immediate aftermath of Devon Loch's collapse she had said, 'Well, that's racing!' – and a few days later she wrote to Devon Loch's trainer Peter Cazalet: 'We will not be done in by this, and will just keep on trying.'

The Queen Mother was never to own a Grand National winner, but the name of Devon Loch lives on as the supreme example of defeat snatched from the jaws of victory.

(Dick Francis's version of events can be found in *The Sport of Queens*, published in 1957.)

DIABLO
The Cisco Kid's horse

Created by O. Henry – better known as the author of

compelling short stories than of a popular television children's western – the series featured the Cisco Kid himself (played by Duncan Renaldo) and his horse, the white-faced and wall-eyed Diablo.

In his eye-catching colourful shirts, silver spurs and suave manner, the Kid was the charmer. By contrast, his sidekick Pancho (Leo Carrillo) is unkempt and overweight, and by way of a comic subplot fights a constant struggle to express himself in English. Pancho's horse also – white-faced and wall-eyed – is Loco.

The Cisco Kid first appeared as a character in the O. Henry story 'The Caballero's Way', published in 1907, followed by a radio series which ran from 1942 to 1955.

A half-hour every week in which the two protagonists right wrongs in the area around the border between the USA and Mexico in the late nineteenth century, accompanied by much joviality, *The Cisco Kid* first aired in September 1950 and ran for 156 episodes, finishing in March 1956.

DIOMED
First Derby winner

Tradition insists – without evidence – that the name of the most famous Flat race in the world derives from a toss of a coin between the twelfth Earl of Derby and his friend Sir Charles Bunbury, at a dinner to celebrate the first running of the Oaks on Epsom Downs in 1779. Wags like to assert that, had the coin fallen the other way, Liverpool would play Everton in the Merseyside Bunbury.

Bunbury may have lost the toss, but he won the first Derby – with his horse Diomed. In all, he owned three Derby winners.

DIOMEDES – mares/horses of
The eighth Labour of Hercules

In classical mythology, Hercules was the son of Zeus and Alkmene – daughter of Elektryon, king of Mycenae, who had acceded to the throne upon the death of his father Perseus, slayer of the Gorgon Medusa.

The same myth can be packaged in all manner of different versions, but in simple terms the story of the Labours – one of the most familiar episodes of classical mythology – come in the shape of a challenge laid down by Eurystheus, king of the Argolid, and performing all twelve will earn Hercules immortality.

The sequence starts with the Menean Lion, followed by the Hydra of Lerna, the Kerynitian Hind, the Erymanthian Boar, the Augean Stables (which accommodate cattle rather than horses), the Stymphalian Birds and the Cretan Bull.

Then come the Horses of Diomedes, set in Thrace.

Diomedes, son of the war-god Ares, is king of one of the Thracian tribes, and has four mares whom he feeds with human flesh, and keeps tethered to bronze mangers with iron chains. All Hercules has to do is liberate the mares and deliver them to Eurystheus. He tames the mares by feeding them the flesh of Diomedes himself, and then taking them back formed into a chariot team.

One variant of the myth has the king setting the captive mares free – and they are torn apart by wild beasts on Mount Olympus.

DONKEYS
'I also had my hour'

Donkeys and asses (the words are interchangeable) have not,

on the whole, had a very good press, and tend to generate cheap laughs. For example, when in the film *Carry On, Follow That Camel*, the well-upholstered Joan Sims asks Phil Silvers as she rides by on her donkey, 'I have a good ass, no?'

G.K. Chesterton showed more respect:

When fishes flew and forests walked
And figs grew upon thorn,
Some moment when the moon was blood
Then surely I was born.

With monstrous head and sickening cry
And ears like errant wings,
The devil's walking parody
On all four-footed things.

The tattered outlaw of the earth,
Of ancient crooked will;
Starve, scourge, deride me: I am dumb,
I keep my secret still.

Fools! For I also had my hour;
One far fierce hour and sweet:
There was a shout about my ears,
And palms before my feet.

DOVER
Eliza Doolittle at the races

In the 1964 movie *My Fair Lady*, based on the George Bernard Shaw play *Pygmalion*, linguist Professor Henry Higgins (played by Rex Harrison) is trying to pass off lowly flower-girl Eliza Doolittle (Audrey Hepburn) as a true aristocrat. He and his friend Colonel Pickering take Eliza to the rarefied atmosphere of the Royal Enclosure at Ascot, where her admirer Freddy Eynsford-Hill has backed a horse named Dover. Freddy gives the ticket to Eliza – 'You'll enjoy the race ever so much more.'

As the race develops, so Eliza's demeanour changes. Fists clenched with excitement, she leans forward to get a better view of the action, and starts to murmur encouragement *sotto voce* – 'Come on, Dover! – and then her inhibitions are cast off as her prim fellow racegoers stare at her in wonder. 'Come on, come on, Dover! Come on, Dover!', she repeats as the ladies and gentlemen around her show their distaste for such behaviour.

As Dover (unseen on the screen) moves into contention, Eliza's encouragement reaches fresh heights: 'Come on, Dover!!! Move yer bloomin' arse!!!'

Bring out the smelling salts for neighbouring racegoers – and sadly, history has not related Dover's finishing position in the race.

DRUMHEAD
Horse who liked a tipple

Politician, *bon viveur* and sporting man Sir John Astley was one of the most attractive equestrian personalities of the nineteenth century. When at a public meeting he was asked his opinion of Sir Wilfrid Lawson's Liquor Bill, which aimed to curtail the consumption of alcohol, Astley reports, 'I pulled myself together and promptly stated that I didn't know much about Sir W. Lawson's Liquor Bill but I did know that *mine* was a deuced sight too high that year'.

A horse named Drumhead had a special place in the Astley

affections – the more so when the combination, with Astley carrying sixteen stone, won a match race at Newmarket:

> Deary me! there was some cheering, and amid roars of laughter we [winning rider and opponent] shook hands. I know I hurried off to the luncheon tent for a glass, for what with the excitement, and the mighty effort of standing up in one's tiny stirrups for a mile and a half, I was real thirsty . . .
>
> Good old Drumhead! He was the very kindest and quietest of horses. I once gave him some whisky before he ran at Shrewsbury, as I thought he didn't struggle quite as gamely as he ought, and the old boy liked the cordial so well, that he followed me round the paddock in hope of another suck at the bottle . . .
>
> To show the mutual confidence that existed between us, I have often sat on his quarters and smoked my baccy whilst he was laying down in the box.

ECLIPSE

'Eclipse first – the rest nowhere'

In 1769 a Smithfield meat salesman named William Wildman arranged a trial between two horses on Banstead Downs, near Epsom. Four years earlier he had bought for 75 guineas a chestnut horse, whom he had allowed to mature. But now that the horse had reached the age of five, it was time to see just how good he was.

Then as now, information about racehorses was the currency of racing, and touts would go to great lengths to gather information. A group made their way to Banstead, where they were alarmed to discover that the trial had already taken place. According to a contemporary report:

> They found an old woman, who gave them all the information

they wanted. On inquiring whether she had seen a race, she replied she could not tell whether it was a race or not, but she had just seen a horse with a white leg running away at a monstrous rate, and another horse a great way behind, trying to run after him; but she was sure he would never catch the white-legged horse if he ran to the world's end.

That 'horse with a white leg' was Eclipse.

Foaled in 1764 and named after the eclipse of the sun which took place on 1 April, the day of the horse's birth, Eclipse was bred by the Duke of Cumberland ('The Butcher of Culloden'), who died in 1765 before the horse ran in a race.

Eclipse's inaugural contest was in heats at Epsom, and the chestnut won the first very easily indeed – at which point an Irish gambler named Dennis O'Kelly declared that he could predict the order of finishing for the next heat. When his challenge was taken up by a fellow gambler, O'Kelly spoke the five words which became part of racing language, and sometimes beyond: 'Eclipse first, the rest nowhere': that is, all the other runners would be 'distanced' by Eclipse, finishing more than 240 yards behind him. O'Kelly was right. He won his bet, and later would buy the horse.

In eighteen races Eclipse was never headed, let alone beaten, and he went on to prove a very influential sire.

He died in 1789.

ELSICH
'The Arkle of awfulness'

In the annals of horseracing, it is not only the winners whose names live on. And in the ranks of multiple losers a special place is reserved for those who have lost often but never won.

There are horses like Peggy's Pet, who posted a record untainted by victory and who between 1962 and 1969 lost ninety-four races – Flat, hurdles and steeplechases. He was also defeated in seventeen point-to-points.

Of more recent memory is Amrullah, who failed to win in seventy-four outings (Flat, hurdles and chases) between 1982 and 1992; whose retirement was covered by national television news; and who won over £25,000 in place money.

Not forgetting **QUIXALL CROSSETT**, who lost in 103 races 'under Rules' and one point-to-point, and has an entry of his own in this book.

Other countries, other losers. In Australia, Ouene boasts 124 defeats without winning, while Japanese racehorse Haru Urara became a national hero of sorts after losing 113 races between 1998 and 2003.

As for the USA, **ZIPPY CHIPPY** also deserves an entry of his own.

There is a special place in the pantheon occupied by the horse dubbed 'The Arkle of Awfulness': Elsich, in some quarters judged the worst horse ever to run in the Grand National, who also ran three times in the Cheltenham Gold Cup. Furthermore, Elsich has the rare distinction of falling twice in the same race – a feat he performed twice.

Owned and bred by Shropshire farmer Charlie Edwards, Elsich was born in 1936, and did not reach a racecourse until February 1945, when he made his debut in a handicap at Cheltenham. He fell early in the race, but Edwards was sufficiently encouraged to bring the horse out again ninety minutes later. He fell again.

Next time out, and again at Cheltenham, Elsich was pulled up, but the ever-optimistic Edwards decided that his pride and joy should run in the Cheltenham Gold Cup in March 1945. Elsich started at 50/1, and ran out at the second fence. Two weeks later he was back at Cheltenham, and fell at the same obstacle.

Elsich had a second crack at the Gold Cup in 1946. Starting at the stingy odds of 200/1, he enjoyed a fleeting minute in the limelight when leading his rivals – among them the winner, the great Prince Regent – from the second fence to the fifth, before rapidly fading out of contention. He got as far as the water jump on the second circuit, where he fell.

Then Elsich broke the habit of a lifetime when getting round without mishap at Worcester. Admittedly he started the 50/1 outsider of three runners, and admittedly he finished a country mile behind his opponents, but in those days completing the course qualified him for the Grand National.

The run-up to the National included two further trips to Cheltenham, on both of which excursions he completed the course. On the first occasion, jockey Bill Balfe got him round after remounting. In his next race he fell two fences from home; was remounted; fell again at the last; was remounted again. (Remounting is not permitted nowadays.)

A 100/1 outsider, Elsich reached the start of the 1946 Grand National without mishap, but did not get very far in the race itself, falling at the first fence.

Then came what was, in Elsich terms, a purple patch, including successive days at Ludlow when he finished in the money: second (of two, beaten out of sight) and third (of three, tailed off).

In the 1947 Cheltenham Gold Cup he started at 100/1 and

was pulled up at the third fence. There was talk of a stirrup leather having broken.

After competing at such lofty heights, Elsich was soon back to his old ways, and when he refused halfway through a race at the now defunct Newport racecourse, the authorities decided that the joke was wearing a bit thin. Entries would no longer be accepted for the horse.

Charlie Edwards was robust in defence of his hero, firing off a letter to the *Sporting Life*, but to no avail.

In all, Elsich ran in fifty races. He fell twenty-three times, pulled up five times and ran out or refused on three more occasions.

But it was not all humiliation: he did earn Edwards £35 in prize money.

See also **QUIXALL CROSSETT** *and* **ZIPPY CHIPPY**

EEYORE
Downbeat donkey in the Winnie-the-Pooh stories

Eeyore – the name replicates the braying of a donkey – has spread gloom over the decades since he first appeared in 1926 in A.A. Milne's *Winnie-the-Pooh*. The word frequently attributed to him is 'pessimistic', but there is more to Eeyore than that. He may not be the brightest spoon in the honey pot, but he takes care to assess an issue from all sides (which takes longer than a quick answer) and is steady and ruminative, happy enough with how he gets on with life.

Pooh-bear and his friends – among them Piglet the piglet, Heffalump the elephant, Kanga the kangaroo and Tigger the tiger – were, for the most part, based on the soft toys who populated the nursery of Milne's son Christopher Robin.

At the opening of chapter 4 we meet a fresh character: 'The old grey donkey, Eeyore, stood by himself in a thistly corner of the Forest, his front feet well apart, and thought about things.' What Eeyore is thinking about is the whereabouts of his tail, which he seems to have mislaid. Pooh – a real friend, says Eeyore, 'Not Like Some' – eventually turns up with the tail, which had been commandeered as a bell-pull at the tree-house of Owl. Christopher Robin nails it back onto Eeyore with a drawing pin, who frolics around the wood in his happiness: a far cry from the gloom-laden donkey.

Eeyore comes centre stage again in chapter 6, 'in which Eeyore had a birthday and gets two presents'; and chapter 8, 'in which Christopher Robin leads an expotition [sic] to the North Pole'. He also features in three later books: *The House at Pooh Corner*, *When We Were Very Young* and *Now We Are Six*. Among the talents he displays, Eeyore is far better than expected at Poohsticks.

EPONA
Horse goddess

In Celtic mythology, Epona is the goddess who protects horses, and is associated with fertility, sexuality and water. She was adopted by the Roman cavalry and celebrated at an annual Roman festival.

EQUUS CABALLUS
Taxonomy of the horse

In the formal, and here streamlined, terms of classification, this is the place of the horse – *Equus caballus* – in the Great Scheme of Things:

Class: Mammalia;
Superorder: Mesaxonia;
Order: Perissodactyla;
Suborder: Hippomorpha;
Family: Equidea;
Genus: Equids;
Species: Mountain Zebra; Plains Zebra; Dolichohippus (Grévy's Zebra); Asinus; Hemionus; Equus Caballus.

Among other relatives of the horse are:

- Hinny: offspring of male horse and female ass;
- Kiang: Asian wild ass;
- Kulan: sub-species of onager;
- Mule: offspring of male ass and female horse;
- Onager: wild ass;
- **QUAGGA**: see entry.

See also **ZEBRA CROSSINGS**

ESCAPE
Eighteenth-century royal racing scandal

As Prince of Wales, Prince Regent and monarch, George IV (1762–1830) was a controversial figure. Eschewing the culture of servility which was to characterise later attitudes to the royal family, the acerbic diarist Charles Greville declared of George, 'A more contemptible, cowardly, selfish, unfeeling dog does not exist', and the close connection of 'Prinny' with horse racing did little to increase trust.

Nor was the sport the only attraction for George at Ascot or Newmarket. An early nineteenth-century satirical print is captioned, 'His royal highness with a lady of quality driving to Ascot races' – when the 'lady of quality' is no such thing.

The most notorious scandal involving George was the so-called 'Escape affair' in October 1791, when the future king was still Prince of Wales.

On 20 October, Escape took part in a two-mile race at Newmarket. Ridden by Sam Chifney – the leading jockey of his time, whose level of self-regard was demonstrated by his entitling his autobiography *Genius Genuine* – Escape started at odds of 1/2 against three opponents. In modern parlance he was a shoo-in, but he managed to finish last of the quartet.

The following day Escape was back in action – this time over four miles against five rivals, two of whom had finished in front of him the previous afternoon. Escape started at 5/1, and guess what: this time he won easily, immediately triggering suspicions that Chifney had 'pulled' Escape in the first race in order to secure a longer price in the second race. (In those days jockeys were not barred from betting.)

The Jockey Club was briskly on the case, with senior steward Sir Charles Bunbury (see **DIOMED**) declaring, 'If Chifney were suffered to ride the Prince's horses, no gentleman would start against him.'

Infuriated by Bunbury's implied threat, the Prince closed down his Newmarket stud, and never returned to the town.

A postscript to the Escape affair came fourteen years after the event, when in 1805 Bunbury and fellow Jockey Club steward the Earl of Darlington wrote to Prinny in conciliatory terms:

From various misconceptions or differences of opinion which arose formerly relative to a race, in which your royal highness was concerned, we greatly regret, that we have never been honoured with your presence there [Newmarket] since that period. But experiencing as we constantly do, the singular marks of your condescension and favour, and considering the essential benefit not only that the Turf will generally derive, but also the great satisfaction that we all must individually feel from the honour of your presence, we humbly request that your royal highness will bury in oblivion any past unfortunate occurrences at Newmarket and you will be pleased to honour us there with your countenance and support.

But the olive branch was declined, and as prince or king, George would never return to Newmarket (though he continued to attend Ascot).

(For a straightforward account of the 'Escape Affair', see Christopher Hibbert, *George IV: Prince of Wales*, published in 1972.)

FALADA
Talking horse in Grimms' fairy tale

'The Goose-Girl' is one of the less familiar tales collected by the Brothers Grimm – Jacob (1785–1863) and Wilhelm (1786–1859) – but Falada has his place in the great tradition of talking equids (such as **BALAAM'S ASS** and **MISTER ED**).

The plot of this brisk story, primarily having a princess traduced by her waiting-maid, has Falada slaughtered and his head cut off and displayed on the city gate. But it takes more than such a grisly end to stop the horse speaking out, and eventually the princess is returned to her rightful position with her prince, and all is resolved. All, that is, except for poor Falada, whose head remains on the city gate.

FLICKA
Multi-talented superstar

Flicka was a horse who acted on a variety of what some might nowadays call 'platforms'.

She first appeared in *My Friend Flicka*, a novel by the American author Mary O'Hara published in 1941. The plot centres around Ken McLaughlin, young son of a rancher in Wyoming, and his close relationship with the skittish filly whom he names Flicka – Swedish for 'little girl'.

The novel formed part of a trilogy, followed as it was by *Thunderhead* (1943) and *Green Grass of Wyoming* (1946).

My Friend Flicka was so well received as a children's story that a film swiftly followed the novel, and the movie was released in 1943, with Roddy McDowall as Ken. This was followed by two sequels based on O'Hara's other novels: *Thunderhead, Son of Flicka* in 1945 and *Green Grass of Wyoming* in 1948.

A radio adaptation of *My Friend Flicka* was broadcast in June 1943, but it was the television series that spread the word most quickly. The programme was first broadcast on the CBS network in the USA in 1956 and in the United Kingdom the following year.

Recent years have witnessed a marked revival of interest in the horse and Ken her soulmate. *Flicka* was released by 20th Century Fox in 2006, with Ken transmogrified to Katy, and this was followed by *Flicka 2* in 2010 and *Flicka: Country Pride* in 2012.

FOINAVON

100/1 winner of a sensational Grand National

Foinavon was the steeplechaser who in 1967 won the biggest race of them all because he was so far behind his rivals at the *moment critique.*

Bred by Anne, Duchess of Westminster, owner of ARKLE, and like that champion named after a mountain on the Duchess's Scottish estate, Foinavon (misspelled from the mountain's name of Foinaven) had proved such a moderate racehorse that he was sold to small-time owner Cyril Watkins for two thousand guineas. He went into training in Berkshire with John Kempton, and his new connections hoped that a change of scene might trigger a change of form.

Some hope. He finished a distant fourth behind Dormant in the 1966 King George VI Chase at Kempton Park (when the injured Arkle hobbled home in what was to prove his final race), and last (at 500/1) in the 1967 Cheltenham Gold Cup. Come the 1967 Grand National he had run twenty-three times for his new connections, without winning. National or no National, neither owner Watkins nor trainer Kempton went to Aintree to watch their horse pursue what was surely an impossible feat. Kempton, who usually rode Foinavon in his races, was too heavy to make the horse's weight at Aintree, and jockey John Buckingham was engaged for the ride.

Foinavon's starting price of 100/1 was distinctly on the niggardly side, and by the time the field reached Becher's Brook on the second circuit, Foinavon was out with the washing, while the leading horses were being towed along by a loose horse named Popham Down, who had been brought down at the first fence and just kept going, now hugging the inside rail.

Approaching the twenty-third fence, the smallest on the circuit, Popham Down decided that he'd had enough fun for one afternoon, and veered sharply to his right to avoid jumping the obstacle. He slammed into other runners – at which point cue Michael O'Hehir, the great Irish commentator, covering that part of the race for BBC television:

> And Rutherfords has been hampered and so has Castle Falls! Rondetto has fallen! Princeful has fallen! Norther has fallen! Kirtle-Lad has fallen! The Fossa has fallen! There's a right pile-up! Leedsy has climbed over the fence and left his jockey there – and now, with all this mayhem, Foinavon has gone off on his own. He's about fifty, a hundred yards in front of everything else . . .

Foinavon had been too far back to be involved in the mayhem, and now, in a bizarre reconstruction of the Tortoise and the Hare, Buckingham calmly took the horse towards the far rail. He popped him over the Canal Turn fence, steered to his left, and set sail for home, with about a mile to gallop and six fences to be jumped.

The favourite Honey End was the only runner to give serious pursuit, but the effort of trying to close the gap proved beyond him. Foinavon came home in glorious isolation, fifteen lengths ahead of his closest pursuer.

There followed a barrage of anger and exasperation that the world's greatest steeplechase should have been reduced to such a farce – this was the time when Aintree racecourse was faced with the distinct prospect of closure – yet a simple truth bears repetition: Foinavon should not have won the 1967 Grand National, but he did.

(An excellent telling of the whole story can be found in *Foinavon: The Story of the Grand National's Biggest Upset* by David Owen, published in 2013.)

FOUR HORSEMEN OF THE APOCALYPSE
Horses at the end of the world

The Revelation of St John the Divine, final book of the New Testament, is one of the most powerful pieces of writing in the Bible. Never mind, for the moment, the vexed issue of interpretation. Just wallow in the power of the prose. The Lamb – God – has a book locked by seven seals:

> And I saw when the Lamb opened one of the seals, and I heard, as it were the noise of thunder, one of the four beasts saying, Come and see.
>
> And I saw, and beheld a white horse: and he that sat on him had a bow; and a crown was given unto him: and he went forth conquering, and to conquer.
>
> And when he had opened the second seal, I heard the second beast say, Come and see.
>
> And there went out another horse that was red: and power was given to him that sat thereon to take peace from the earth, and that they should kill one another: and there was given unto him a great sword.
>
> And when he had opened the third seal, I heard the third beast say, Come and see. And I beheld, and lo a black horse; and he that sat on him had a pair of balances in his hand.
>
> And I heard a voice in the midst of the four beasts say, A

measure of wheat for a penny, and three measures of barley for a penny; and see thou hurt not the oil and the wine.

And when he had opened the fourth seal, I heard the voice of the fourth beast say, Come and see.

And I looked, and behold a pale horse: and his name that sat upon him was Death, and Hell followed with him. And power was given unto them over the fourth part of the earth, to kill with sword, and with hunger, and with death, and with the beasts of the earth.

In summary, the horseman in white is Christ the Conqueror; the horseman in red is War; the horseman in black is Famine; and the pale horse is Plague.

Later in Revelation comes this passage:

And I saw heaven opened, and behold a white horse; and he that sat upon him was called Faithful and True, and in righteousness he doth judge and make war.

His eyes were as a flame of fire, and on his head were many crowns; and he had a name written, that no man knew, but he himself.

And he was clothed with a vesture dipped in blood: and his name is called The Word of God.

And the armies which were in heaven followed him upon white horses, clothed in fine linen, white and clean.

Of particular interest is the white horse, who has considerable iconographic force. In T.S. Eliot's poem 'The Journey of the Magi', an old white horse gallops away in the meadow, prefiguring the return of Christ on Judgement Day. There are several white horses cut into the landscape of the British Isles: see **UFFINGTON WHITE HORSE**.

FOXHUNTER
Fabled showjumper

On the Blorenge mountain in Wales is a memorial plaque which reads:

FOXHUNTER
23rd April 1940 – 21st November 1959
Here lies FOXHUNTER
Champion International Show Jumper
Winner of 78 International Competitions
including many foreign Grand Prix and the
King George V Gold Cup 1948, 1950 and 1953
35 times member of the British Show Jumping Team
which won Olympic Gold Medals at Helsinki, 1952
Bronze Medals at [Olympics] London, 1948
Prince of Wales Cup, London, five times (1949–1953)
and the Aga Khan Cup outright, Dublin (1950, 1951, 1953)

What this roll of honour could not encapsulate was the affection – the genuine love – which this bay gelding attracted among the general public. In a golden age of British showjumping, Foxhunter – owned and ridden by Harry Llewellyn, who had finished runner-up in the 1936 Grand National – was the poster boy.

The memorial stone lists the achievements, but cannot describe the drama behind them – notably in the case of the 1952 Olympics at Helsinki. Late in the games, Great Britain had yet to achieve a single entry in the gold-medal column. The one serious remaining chance was in the showjumping team event, but after the first round GB was back in fifth place. It all came down to this: Foxhunter and Llewellyn had to get round with no more than a single fence down. Cometh the hour, cometh the horse – and Foxhunter turned in a brilliant clear round to secure the gold medals.

FRANKEL
Greatest ever horse on the Flat?

'Comparisons', according to Dogberry in *Much Ado About Nothing*, 'are odorous'. But the compulsion among followers of horse racing to compare one horse with another runs deep, and by some measures – including simple gut feelings – Frankel, born in 2008, was the best horse ever to have raced on the Flat in Europe.

A son of the 2001 Derby winner Galileo, Frankel was bred and owned by Prince Khalid Abdullah (of Saudi Arabia), trained at Newmarket by the late Sir Henry Cecil and ridden in all of his fourteen races by Tom Queally.

Frankel's unblemished career was played out against the subplot of Sir Henry's terminal illness. Long acclaimed as one of the finest trainers of all, through Frankel's three-season career Cecil seemed to be staving off the inevitable, as he became ever more spectral in appearance – notably when Frankel put up one of the greatest performances of all at York as a four-year-old, when he demolished a top-class field.

In summary:

Frankel won all four of his races as a two-year-old in 2010 (including the Dewhurst Stakes, top two-year-old race of the year); all his five races as a three-year-old (including a barnstorming performance to land the Two Thousand Guineas by six lengths); and all five as a four-year-old, culminating in victory in the Champion Stakes at Ascot.

Ten of those races were designated Group 1 – the elite level in European racing.

For decades the Halifax-based Timeform organisation has led the field in the dissemination of racing form, and at the end of the 2012 season assessed Frankel on a mark of 147 pounds. The previous highest rating was 145, awarded to the brilliant Sea Bird, in 1965 winner of the Derby and Prix de l'Arc de Triomphe.

(*Frankel*, edited by Andrew Pennington and published in 2012, is a profusely illustrated summing up of a great career.)

FROU-FROU
Ill-fated steeplechaser in Anna Karenina

'All happy families are alike; each unhappy family is unhappy in its own way.' The opening sentence of Leo Tolstoy's novel *Anna Karenina*, first published in book form in Russia in 1878, sets the mood for a tale of some very unhappy families. Married to a government official many years her elder, the eponymous countess Anna falls under the spell of the dashing Count Vronsky, with inevitable results.

One of the great set-pieces of a novel which Dostoyevsky called a 'flawless work of art' is the steeplechase in which Vronsky takes part.

This is not the place for analysis of all the intrigues and emotions swirling around the racecourse. Better just to sample one of most graphic pieces of horse writing in European literature. After running neck-and-neck with his main rival Mahotin, Vronsky on Frou-Frou has taken the lead.

There remained only the last ditch, filled with water and five feet wide. Vronsky did not even look at it, but anxious to get in a long way first began sawing away at the reins, lifting the mare's head and letting it go in time with her paces. He felt that the mare was at her very last reserve of strength; not her neck and shoulders merely were wet, but the sweat was standing in drops on her mane, her head, her sharp ears, and her breath came in short, sharp gasps. But he knew that she had strength left more than enough for the remaining five hundred yards.

It was only from feeling himself nearer the ground and from the peculiar smoothness of his motion that Vronsky knew how greatly the mare had quickened her pace. She flew over the ditch as though not noticing it. She flew over it like a bird; but at the same instant Vronsky, to his horror, felt that he had failed to keep up with the mare's pace, that he had, he did not know how, made a fearful, unpardonable mistake, in recovering his seat in the saddle. All at once his position had shifted and he knew that something awful had happened. He could not yet make out what had happened, when the white legs of a chestnut horse flashed by close to him, and Mahotin passed at a swift gallop. Vronsky was touching the ground with one foot, and his mare was sinking on that foot. He just had time to free his leg when she fell on one side, gasping painfully, and, making vain efforts to rise with her delicate, soaking neck, she fluttered on the ground at his feet like a shot bird. The clumsy movement made by Vronsky had broken her back. But that he only knew much later. At that moment he knew only that Mahotin had flown swiftly by, while he stood staggering alone on the muddy, motionless ground, and Frou-Frou lay gasping before him, bending her head back and gazing at him with her exquisite eyes.

Still unable to realize what had happened, Vronsky tugged at his mare's reins. Again she struggled all over like a fish, and her shoulders setting the saddle heaving, she rose on her front legs but, unable to lift her back, she quivered all over and again fell on her side. With a face hideous with passion, his lower jaw trembling, and his cheeks white, Vronsky kicked her with his heel in the stomach and again fell to tugging at the rein. She did not stir, but thrusting her nose into the ground, she simply gazed at her master with her speaking eyes.

A horrified Vronsky leaves the racecourse immediately. 'For the first time in his life,' Tolstoy writes, 'he knew the bitterest kind of misfortune – misfortune beyond remedy, caused by his own fault.'

FUJIYAMA CREST
Final leg of Frankie Dettori's 'Magnificent Seven'

Ascot, 28 September 1996. By the time jockey Frankie Dettori left the Ascot weighing room for his seventh and final ride of the day, that sometimes staid racecourse had worked itself into a lather of excitement. For on the day of the Festival of British Racing, a showcase for the sport of horse racing at the highest level, Dettori had won all six races that had been run: in chronological order the winners were Wall Street, Diffident, Mark Of Esteem, Decorated Hero, Fatefully and Lochangel.

Enter a hitherto obscure four-year-old gelding named Fujiyama Crest, top weight in the concluding race of the day, the Gordon Carter Handicap over two miles. Fujiyama Crest had won this race the previous year, but had not shown very good form earlier in 1996, and his price on the morning of the Ascot race was understandably around 12/1.

Those odds represented Fujiyama Crest's chance on interpretation of the form book, but as Dettori steered his mount towards the two-mile start, the form book had become redundant. Bookmakers had spent much of the afternoon happily accepting combination bets on Dettori's rides, secure in the knowledge that the sequence could not possibly continue. Now, after six winners of six races, some bookies were bearing huge liabilities, and had to limit the damage as best they could – and that meant making Fujiyama Crest a very short price. He started at 2/1, and despite the pessimism suggested by the form book, battled up the straight to win by a neck from Pat Eddery on Northern Fleet, to trigger wild champagne-soaked scenes of celebration of one of the great riding feats: no jockey had ever 'gone through' a seven-race card.

Then came the stories of the punters and the bookies: some had sizeable wins, others lost catastrophically, some just missed out.

The cumulative odds about the seven winners came to 25,095/1. Many punters won big, and some won very big indeed: like Darren Yates of Morecambe, who won £550,823.54 for an outlay of £67.58.

But spare a thought for cleaner Pat Epton, who had a 50 pence single bet on each of Frankie's seven rides, and won £14.66. Had she staked another 50 pence on an accumulator on the seven, she would have won an additional £12,047.50.

And spare another thought for bookmaker Gary Wiltshire, who – convinced as he was that Fujiyama Crest was starting at a ridiculous price – 'stood' many bets rather than lay off with other bookies, and ended up selling his house in order to clear his debts.

As for Fujiyama Crest, he was retired from racing in July 2000. Later that year his erstwhile groom, Derek Heeney, was at Sandown Park racecourse when he bumped into Frankie Dettori, who asked how 'the old horse' was. The result of that conversation was that Frankie bought Fujiyama Crest as a hack for his wife Catherine, declaring that since the horse had made him famous, giving him a home for the rest of his life was the least he could do. 'He was more than a pet,' said Frankie after Fujiyama Crest had died in 2015. 'He was a part of the family.'

FUM
First mount for Princess Anne

'Once upon a time there was a small girl of two-ish, who was placed on an almost equally small bundle of cream hair called Fum,' begins *Riding through My Life* by the Princess Royal (born 1950). 'What followed was a direct result of that apparently successful encounter and of being born into a family of talented equestrians (horse riders), brought up in a lifestyle in which the horse played an integral part.' The 'what followed' to which she alludes was a career as a leading international three-day eventer and enthusiastic amateur race rider, both on the Flat and over jumps.

She first competed at the Badminton Horse Trials in 1971 on Doublet, finishing fifth, and later that year won the European Three-Day Event Championships at Burghley on the same horse: 'To receive the prize from my mother and the medal from my father on a horse bred by my mother was very special, but I don't think I realised *how* special until I understood more about the difficulties of breeding an event horse and getting it prepared and chosen to run in an international competition, never mind winning it.' She competed in the British team in the 1976 Olympic Games in Montreal, thereby becoming the first member of the British Royal Family to represent the country at an Olympiad.

Princess Anne rode in her first horse race under Jockey Club Rules on Against The Grain at Epsom in April 1983, had her first winner on the Flat on Gulfland at Redcar in August 1986 and in all won five Flat races in Britain, including the Dresden Diamond Stakes at Ascot – then the most prestigious ladies' race in the calendar – in July 1987 on Ten No Trumps and the Queen Mother Cup (named for her grandmother) at York on Insular in June 1988. 'Insular knows more about racing than I do,' she said afterwards. 'I just sat on him and let him get on with it.' She started riding over jumps in March 1985 and had her only steeplechase winner on Cnoc-Na-Cuille at Worcester in September 1987.

In 1983 she became President of the British Olympic Association and in 1986 President of the Fedération Equestre Internationale (FEI). Among her many other equestrian activities, she has been Master of the Worshipful Company of Farriers and Honorary Freeman of the Worshipful Company of Saddlers, and has been closely involved in the work of the Riding for the Disabled Association. She is also Patron of the Injured Jockeys' fund.

Princess Anne, who became the Princess Royal in 1987, was once reported to have observed: 'The horse is about the only person who does not know you are royal.'

FURY

Black stallion in the television series

While not quite the equal of **CHAMPION THE WONDER HORSE** in public esteem, Fury was a highly popular weekly series between its first broadcast in October 1955 and its last in March 1960. The stories were based on a simple premise similar to that of Champion: boy – in this case Joey Newton – has adventures with horse. The nature of these stories is established by the episode names: 'Joey Finds a Friend', 'Joey Saves the Day', 'Joey Sees It Through', 'Joey Shows the Way', and so on.

An extra dimension to the series concept is that Fury – who sports a white star on his forehead – is a wild stallion, and with rare exceptions will allow no one other than the orphan Joey to ride him.

The 'real' Fury was a purebred American Saddlebred horse named Highland Dale, who in addition to his television duties appeared in several movies, including the 1946 version of *Black Beauty*.

GABILAN
Steinbeck's red pony

John Steinbeck's sometimes wistful, sometimes brutal story 'The Red Pony' was first published in three parts in 1937, as part of a collection of stories under the title *The Long Valley*. 'The Gift' describes how Jody Tiflin is given the chestnut pony, and the moral responsibility which comes with him. 'The Great Mountains' is mostly concerned with the issues of old age. And 'The Promise' describes Jody's relationship with the colt bought to replace Gabilan.

Steinbeck (1902–1968), who was awarded the Nobel Prize for Literature in 1962, produced a memorable piece of equine writing after making his first visit to the Kentucky Derby in Louisville in 1956 – a 'place of pilgrimage' which sees him reflecting that if the national elections took place on Derby

Day, 'our next president would be a horse'. (In Ireland, Arkle was likewise suggested as a presidential candidate. See page 13.)

At the Derby, he rightly appreciates that horses are the major players in this totemic event: 'They are just plain beautiful. They may well be the most beautiful thing in the world. I wish we could improve our breed as we have improved theirs'.

Later he notes how the runners in the big race are 'sleek and memorable, perfect as birds, specialised as snakes'.

Another great American novelist to have written lyrically about the Kentucky Derby is William Faulkner (1897-1962), whose report from the 1955 running includes the observation that 'what the horse supplies to man is something deep and profound in his emotional nature and need'.

GALGO JR
Record winner

Galgo Jr is the horse with the most wins in racing history. Between 1930 and 1936 he won no fewer than 137 races in his native Puerto Rico, and in all he ran 159 times and was unplaced only once. At the time of his death – of a heart attack in his box at Monjas Racing Park in December 1936 – he was the holder or joint-holder of eight track records for native Puerto Rican-bred horses.

GATO
Creole horse on 'Tschiffely's Ride'

See **MANCHA AND GATO**

GODOLPHIN
Founding Thoroughbred stallion

See BYERLEY TURK

GOLDEN MILLER (and Dorothy Paget)
High-achieving steeplechaser and his eccentric owner

Golden Miller, born near Dublin in 1927 and sold very cheaply as a yearling at public auction, boasted a remarkable racing record.

He won the Cheltenham Gold Cup five times in a row – 1932 to 1936 – and remains the only horse ever to have won the Gold Cup and Grand National in the same year: 1934. In all he won twenty-nine of his fifty-five races.

But if Golden Miller's feats were extraordinary, so were the habits of his owner: the highly unusual Dorothy Paget.

Outstandingly rich and exceptionally capricious, she had extensive racing interests, both as an owner and as a punter – all financed by the vast fortune she had inherited at the age of twenty.

In addition to Golden Miller, she owned top-class horses such as the brilliant Insurance (Champion Hurdle winner in 1932 and 1933); two other Champion Hurdle winners in the shape of Solford (1940) and Distel (1946); Straight Deal, who won the Derby in 1943, when the premier Classic was run at Newmarket; and two more Cheltenham Gold Cup winners in Roman Hackle (1940) and Mont Tremblant (1952).

In her younger days she had been an accomplished horsewoman, riding side-saddle in point-to-points, but the eccentricity soon got the better of her.

Tucked away in her rambling mansion near Chalfont St Giles in Buckinghamshire, she would sleep during the day and put away huge meals in the middle of the night or the early morning, and have breakfast at 8.30 p.m.

Naturally this sort of lifestyle made communication with the outside world tricky, to say the least, and the trainers of her substantial band of horses found her an exasperating owner.

She was a punter to a gigantic degree – her largest wager in 1930 was reputed to have been £160,000 on the nose of an 8/1 *on* chance – and her unusual daily routine was accommodated by her main bookmaker in a highly unorthodox scheme: she would phone through her bets in the evening, after racing had finished, and wager on races that had already taken place.

Stories of Dorothy Paget's eccentricity are legion, but few are as appealing as the one about the day her car broke down when she was being driven to the races by her secretary. The only other vehicle in sight was a butcher's van, which she instructed her secretary to purchase there and then – and completed her journey to the racecourse sitting between carcasses of meat. Thereafter she went to the races with a second car following as back-up – and for long journeys, a third car.

Dorothy Paget was fifty-four years old when she died in 1960.

(The best biography is by Graham Sharpe and Declan Colley: *Dorothy Paget: The Eccentric Queen of the Sport of Kings*, published in 2017.)

GOVERNATORE
Henry VIII's favourite horse

Henry VIII was a keen horseman, enthusiastically pursuing all manner of equestrian activities, notably jousting, hunting and racing.

'Henry was literally obsessed with jousting,' declared historian Alison Weir. 'He trained regularly, often charging with his lance to dislodge a detachable ring from a post, or tilting at the quintain, a dummy on a revolving bar.' But jousting was a notoriously risky pursuit, and he twice suffered serious injuries.

On Henry's devotion to hunting – the quarry was usually deer – Weir notes Henry's passion for the chase, and cites contemporary state papers: 'He never takes his diversion without tiring eight or ten horses, which he causes to be stationed beforehand along the line of country he means to take, and when one is tired, he mounts another, and before he gets home they are all exhausted.'

He also enjoyed racing his horses against those of his courtiers, and even laid out a racecourse, at Cobham.

In a constant attempt to improve his bloodstock, Henry founded studs – notably at Hampton Court – and at any one time might have been in possession of two hundred horses, of which his favourite bloodlines were the Barbary horses from Spain and Neapolitans from Italy.

As far as individual horses are concerned, the candidates for the top slot in Henry's affections appear to have been Governatore and Canicida, with the verdict – to judge from published sources – going to the former, a bright bay horse given to Henry in 1514 by the notable breeder Francesco

Gonzaga, Marquis of Mantua. Having seen Governatore through his paces, he asked the assembled courtiers whether they had ever seen a better horse. In his opinion, Governatore was 'the best horse', and as he patted his newly acquired prize of Governatore and three broodmares, he supposedly murmured: 'So-ho, so-ho, my minion.' And Henry's thank-you letter to Gonzaga left no doubt about his gratitude, 'for your supreme goodwill towards ourself, for those most beautiful, high-bred and surpassing steeds [that] have been sent from the very best feeling and intention'.

Clearly, a gift of a few well-bred horses was the quickest way to Henry's heart.

(*Henry VIII: King and Court* by Alison Weir, published in 2001, is rich in detail.)

GRANE
Brünnhilde's horse

Richard Wagner's monumental quartet of operas – collectively *Der Ring des Nibelungen* – consists of *Das Rheingold*, *Die Walküre*, *Siegfried* and *Götterdämmerung*, and was first staged as a complete cycle in 1876.

Grane, most celebrated of operatic equines, first appears with Brünnhilde early in *Die Walküre*, and is last seen in the apocalyptic, fire-fuelled climax to *Götterdämmerung*.

Brünnhilde addresses death: 'Hia yoho! Grane, greet your master' – just before confronting one of the more trying exits in the operatic cannon. 'She jumps on the horse,' reads Wagner's stage direction, 'and leaps, with a single bound, into the burning pyre.' The stage is then engulfed by flames. (Do not try this at home.)

The original Grane was described by the *Oxford Dictionary of Opera* as 'a gentle and nimble-footed nine-year-old' who, in the words of the celebrated Wagner critic Ernest Newman, unlike the horse's human co-performers, 'never whined, never stormed, never sulked'.

Given the obvious problems of staging, nowadays some directors have resisted the temptation to have a live horse on stage, relying instead on such devices as imagining Grane off-stage.

Der Ring is not the only opera to require onstage – or within shouting distance off-stage – horses.

The opera critic Hugh Vickers experienced an eventful performance of Mussorgsky's *Boris Godunov* at the Royal Opera House, Covent Garden, in 1958. 'On this occasion,' recorded Vickers, 'Covent Garden had obviously grasped the point that a very large Yugoslav tenor requires a very large horse; indeed I have never seen so vast an animal outside the Yorkshire hunting field.' The Covent Garden audience was mesmerised, and afforded this equine giant rapturous applause after one of the main arias – at which point the horse expressed himself in the only way he knew how, 'and in very large measure.'

In Norse mythology, Grani is a horse owned by the hero Sigurd.

(For more information see the Grane entry in the *Oxford Dictionary of Opera* by John Warrack and Ewan West, published in 1992.)

GRINGOLET
Sir Gawain's horse

In Arthurian legend, Gringolet is the horse upon whom Sir Gawain – usually considered inferior only to Sir Lancelot as a senior knight of the Round Table – pursues his exploits. The best-known treatment of Gawain is the Middle English romance *Sir Gawain and the Green Knight*, completed around 1375, the sole text of which is in the British Library in London, though the name is given to Gawain's horse in versions of the story as early as the twelfth century.

The Green Knight's horse is not named and is green all over, much to the astonishment of Arthur's knights. In modern translation:

> *Such a horse, such a horseman, in the whole wide world*
> *Was never seen or observed by those assembled before,*
> *Not one.*

As for Arthur himself, the horse with whom he is most closely associated is the Welsh-bred mare Llamrei.

(The Penguin Classics edition of *Sir Gawain and the Green Knight*, with translation by Brian Stone, was first published in 1959. A more recent – and more poetic – translation by Simon Armitage was published in 2009.)

HAIZUM
Archangel Gabriel's horse

In Islamic tradition, **HAIZUM** is a white horse with wings (comparisons with Pegasus are obvious) who can fly instantly from one cosmic plane to another – a useful attribute to have.

HAVERLAND
'I love proving people wrong about what a Muslim girl can do'

Khadijah Mellah has a rare distinction: she was the first person to ride the winner of a horse race in Great Britain while wearing a hijab. The story of how eighteen-year-old Khadijah, born and raised on a suburban estate, learned to ride at the Ebony Horse Club in Brixton, then in 2019 narrowly landed the Magnolia Cup at Goodwood on 25/1 chance Haverland, weeks after first riding a racehorse, is one of the most beguiling sporting tales of recent years.

HENRY THE HORSE
Only named horse to feature in a Lennon–McCartney lyric

Early in 1967 the Beatles were in Kent, making the surreal film which accompanied the song 'Strawberry Fields Forever'. In an antique shop in Knole, John Lennon's eye was caught by an 1843 poster advertising a performance of Pablo Fanque's Circus Royal in Rochdale, Lancashire, among whose performers was a horse named Zanthus. The circus was advertised as 'being for the benefit of Mr Kite', which phrase provided the title for the song on *Sgt. Pepper's Lonely Hearts Club Band* in which (of course) Henry the Horse dances the waltz.

HERCULES
The Steptoes' horse

One of the truly great creations of British comedy, *Steptoe and Son* – written by Alan Galton and Ray Simpson – chronicled the lives of rag-and-bone man Albert Steptoe (played by Wilfrid Brambell) and his son Harold (Harry H. Corbett) from 1962 to 1974. For much of that period the third established character in the series was Hercules: an unkempt carthorse, bay with a large white blaze, as shabby as the human inhabitants of Oil Drum Lane – though Albert reveals that Hercules had been Carthorse of the Year at the Acton Gymkhana in 1937.

Hercules had no speaking lines, but proved the centre of attention in 'A Death in the Family', broadcast in 1964.

The episode begins just after Hercules has collapsed in the

street, having suffered a fatal heart attack, and Harold has to break the terrible news to his father, who takes it very badly; even worse when he learns that Harold has sold the faithful horse to the knackers' yard for 'thirty bob' – £1.50 in modern money.

The distraught Albert wails that he had reserved a place for Hercules at the animal cemetery, and instead the horse would wind up on a plate in a Belgian restaurant – or as cat-food in tins (collect three tokens and exchange them for a Freddie and the Dreamers disc).

In more wistful mood, Albert reminisces that Hercules – forty-one years old at his demise in the radio version – had been born on the same day as Princess Margaret, and would have been named Margaret Rose had he been a filly.

Later, Harold reveals he has been to Southall market and bought a horse to replace Hercules. He is planning to name the newcomer 'Samson'.

Meanwhile, the bereaved Albert has not eaten for three days and has taken to his bed – from which he is persuaded to rise by Harold insisting that the newcomer Samson is showing signs of severe illness. Albert examines the stricken horse, and pours scorn on his uninformed son – 'Ya great pillock!'

Samson is not ill but pregnant. Renamed Delilah, she is delivered of a foal, who is called Hercules the Second.

HI-HAT

Hero of Marx Brothers film A Day at the Races

Released in 1937, *A Day at the Races* has long been one of the most popular Marx Brothers movies, and it is not hard to see why.

It has the lot. Groucho, Chico and Harpo are on top form as, respectively, Dr Hugo Z. Hackenbush (masquerading as a medical doctor when in reality he is a horse doctor), Tony and Stuffy. The splendid Margaret Dumont is characteristically overbearing as rich widow Mrs Emily Upjohn, while Gil Stewart (played by crooner Allan Jones) and Judy Standish (Maureen O'Sullivan) provide the love interest.

There are sumptuous production numbers, such as the lavish Gala Water Carnival, at which Harpo plays the harp and Chico the piano in their inimitable styles, but much more fun are the comedy routines. Best of these is the racecourse scene in which Tony sells to Hackenbush an envelope tipping a runner in the next race. It transpires that the contents of that envelope can make sense only if he buys the code book, the contents of which can make sense only if he buys the master code book, the contents of which make sense only if he buys the breeders' guide . . .

Hi-Hat himself appears throughout the film, kicking out in rage when encountering the villain of the piece, Morgan, who insists that 'I should have plugged that nag when I owned him!' Having eluded the clutches of Morgan and his henchmen, the horse escapes by leaping nimbly over a barn door, demonstrating that he is not a horse for the Flat but a jumper, thus setting up the climax of the film. With Stuffy in the saddle, Hi-Hat runs in the Grand Steeplechase at Sparkling Springs.

The race produces too many shenanigans to be listed here, but Hi-Hat wins the race (though not before an irregularity concerning mud obscuring two runners' number-cloths) and the film ends with a triumphal procession, the massed choirs singing about tomorrow being another day, and Hackenbush confessing to Mrs Upjohn: 'I really am a horse doctor. But marry me, and I'll never look at any other horse.'

(Hi-Hat is not to be confused with Sir Winston Churchill's top-class racehorse of the same-sounding name but different spelling, High Hat. See page 68.)

HORACE HORSECOLLAR
Mickey Mouse's friend

Horace Horsecollar was an anthropomorphic black cartoon horse, a popular minor character in early Mickey Mouse movies. Created in 1929 by Ub Iwerks and Walt Disney, Horace made his first appearance with Mickey Mouse in *The Plow Boy*, released in 1929, where he has the role of one of the great mouse's best friends. He soon became a staple of Disney cartoons, appearing alongside such legends as Clara Cluck and Clarabelle Cow. His film appearances include *The Barnyard Concert* (1930) and *Mickey's Mellerdrammer* (1933).

Recently, he has had more sophisticated cameo roles in movies, including *Who Framed Roger Rabbit?* (1988) and *The Prince and the Pauper* (1990).

Horace Horsecollar also had an active life in video games and in comics, frequently teaming up with Clarabelle Cow. The couple's engagement was announced, but they seem not to have gone ahead with wedding plans.

HORSE
. . . who accompanies the boy, the mole and the fox

An engaging piece of whimsy, *The Boy, the Mole, the Fox and the Horse* by Charlie Mackesy was the UK publishing sensation of 2019. Like the other three characters, the Horse delivers a succession of philosophical nuggets, such as:

> Everyone is a bit scared, but we are less scared together.

or

> Tears fall for a reason and they are your strength not weakness.

or

> Sometimes just getting up and carrying on is brave and magnificent.

Towards the end of the book, the Horse reveals: 'I can fly. But I stopped because it made other horses jealous.' To which the boy replies: 'Well we love you whether you can fly or not.'

HOUYHNHNMS
The horse people in Gulliver's Travels

The Houyhnhnms inhabit the fourth and final part of Jonathan Swift's *Gulliver's Travels*, 'A Voyage to the Country of the Houyhnhnms', which was published in 1726 and has remained a classic of satire ever since.

By the time he encounters the Houyhnhnms, Lemuel Gulliver has visited Lilliput in Part I; Brobdingnag in Part II; Laputa, Balnibarbi, Glubbdubdrib, Luggnagg and Japan in Part III, returning home to England in April 1710.

Later that year he boards ship again and sets sail from Portsmouth, and in May 1711 is the victim of a mutiny. He is put down on a remote island and left to fend for himself.

He is soon surrounded by a horde of strange-looking animals, who seem about to attack him – then of a sudden they run away. Gulliver wonders what has caused their hasty departure.

But looking on my left hand, I saw a horse walking softly in the field, which my persecutors having sooner discovered, was the cause of their flight. The horse started a little when he came near me, but soon recovering himself, looked full in my face with manifest tokens of wonder: he viewed my hands and feet, walking round me several times. I would have pursued my journey, but he placed himself directly in the way, yet looking with a very mild aspect, never offering the least violence. We stood gazing at each other for some time; at last I took the boldness to reach my hand towards his neck, with a design to stroke it using the common style and whistle of jockeys when they are going to handle a strange horse. But this animal, seeming to receive my civilities with disdain, shook his head, and bent his brows, softly raising up his left fore-foot to remove my hand. Then he neighed three or four times, but in so different a cadence, that I almost began to think he was speaking to himself in some language of his own.

While he and I were thus employed, another horse came up; who applying himself to the first in a very formal manner, they gently struck each other's right foot before, neighing several times by turn, and varying the sounds, which seemed to be almost articulate. They went some paces off, as if it were to confer together, walking side by side, backward and forward, like persons deliberating on some affair of weight, but often turning their eyes towards me, as it were to watch that I might not escape. I was amazed to see such actions and behaviour in brute beasts, and concluded with myself, that if the inhabitants of this country were endued with a proportionable degree of reason, they must needs be the wisest people on earth.

These horses are far from 'brute beasts'. They are Houyhnhnms – the name echoes the equine whinny – and they are indeed the wisest creatures on earth. And the deformed humanoid animals who had surrounded Gulliver are Yahoos.

Gulliver is taken in by a senior Houyhnhnm whom he comes to call 'my master', and among whose servants is a 'sorrel nag' – a horse of low breeding. He gradually learns about the perfect society lived by the talking horses – 'Friendship and benevolence are the two principal virtues among the Houyhnhnms' – in contrast with the conditions under which the subservient Yahoos live a cruder existence.

Eventually the Assembly of the Houyhnhnms decide that Gulliver too closely resembles a Yahoo to be permanently accommodated by his master, and he has to leave the island. He builds a boat, and on the day of his departure he is seen off:

> My master and his friends continued on the shore, till I was almost out of sight; and I often heard the sorrel nag (who always loved me) crying out, *Hnuy illa nyha maiah Yahoo*, Take care of thyself, gentle Yahoo.

On his return to London, Gulliver finds it difficult to adjust as a Yahoo, and for five years cannot tolerate the smell of his wife and children. To produce a more congenial domestic atmosphere, he buys two horses, and employs a groom:

> I feel my spirits revived by the smell he contracts in the stable. My horses understand tolerably well; I converse with them at least four hours every day. They are strangers to bridle or saddle; they live in great amity with me, and friendship to each other.

IDAHO GEM and PROMETEA
Cloning mules and horses

On 30 May 2003, *The Times* newspaper carried a story which
began:

> A cloned mule has been born in the United States, proving
> that it is possible to clone members of the horse family and
> hybrid animals that cannot normally reproduce.
>
> The birth of Idaho Gem, on 4 May at the University of
> Idaho's Northwest Equine Reproduction Laboratory, could
> lead to the cloning of champion horses and endangered
> species that have difficult breeding on their own.
>
> The success is the culmination of five years of research,
> which had to overcome two major obstacles. First, the mule
> is a hybrid animal, a cross between a female horse and a

male donkey, or jack, and is sterile except in extremely rare
cases . . .

The equine family as a whole has also proved to be a
major challenge to reproductive science, with even in-vitro
fertilisation of horses, let alone cloning, proving elusive.

That challenge had been exercising a team in Italy, and a few
days after the birth of Idaho Gem, on 7 August, the *Independent*
had the story:

> Scientists have created the world's first clone of a horse,
> raising the prospect of genetic copies being made of
> champion thoroughbreds.
>
> A team of Italian veterinary researchers said yesterday
> that the foal, called Prometea, was born naturally on 28 May
> to a surrogate mare who also provided the genetic material
> for the cloning process.
>
> So Prometea has made scientific history twice – for being
> the first horse clone and for being the only cloned animal
> to be born by a surrogate mother which was also a genetic
> twin.
>
> The researchers said the experiment showed that, in
> theory, it would be possible to 'breed' from geldings –
> castrated stallions – that would otherwise be excluded from
> contributing to a bloodstock line.

'In theory' – aye, there's the rub, and the immediate reaction
from spokesmen for equine institutions was less than excited.
Philip Freedman, chairman of the Thoroughbred Breeders'
Association in the UK, considered the development as having
'no value' for the sport, because horses created by artificial
insemination could not enter racing stud books.

INCITATUS
Caligula's horse

Gaius Caligula (reigned AD 37–41) was one of the more comprehensively unhinged Roman emperors, and his eccentricity famously found its dottiest expression in his relationship with his favourite horse, Incitatus. (The name means 'swift'.)

The prime source for information on the horse comes from the historian Suetonius, who in *The Twelve Caesars* (AD 121) related that on the day of horse races in Rome, Caligula stationed troops in the vicinity of the stadium, charged with enforcing absolute silence in order to keep Incitatus calm and collected before the sports began.

Further signals of the emperor's obsession with the horse were the ivory stall in the marble stable in which Incitatus was accommodated, his purple blankets and jewelled halter, and having his own house, furniture and slaves. It was rumoured that Caligula intended to make Incitatus a consul, though there is no evidence that this took place.

A source later than Suetonius, the historian Cassius Dio (AD 155–235), added details such as the horse's feed consisting of oats with gold flake mixed in, and that Caligula made Incitatus a priest.

Suetonius also describes Julius Caesar's charger, named Pascasas in some sources, each of whose hooves were cloven into five parts, as with the human skeleton. Julius Caesar was the first to ride the horse, who subsequently would allow no one else on his back.

JOEY
War horse

Michael Morpurgo's *War Horse* has been a phenomenal success in its various incarnations.

In very brief terms, the novel tells in the horse's voice how, early in the First World War, a boy named Albert falls in love with a horse named Joey; how Joey is sold to assist the army in the war effort, joining a unit of mounted infantry in France; how Joey is captured by the Germans; pulls an ambulance cart; works on the land; is wounded in no-man's-land; is reunited with Albert, who is working in the veterinary hospital; and returns with Albert to England, where they live in peace.

Ostensibly a book for children, *War Horse* was generally very well received upon first publication in 1982. But it was only when a stage version by Nick Stafford opened in London in 2007 that it started to enjoy cult status. That change was in large measure due to the prominent role played by full-size equine models created by the Handspring Puppet Company. These were astounding creations, replicating equine movements with uncanny accuracy, and they triggered a worldwide demand for productions – starting with a transfer to Broadway.

War Horse achieved another major landmark with the release of the Steven Spielberg-directed movie in December 2011, which used real horses.

The statistics regarding equine casualties in the First World War are mind-boggling. It has been estimated that no fewer than 256,000 horses were lost on the Western Front alone – and only 58,000 of those were killed by enemy fire. Over two and a half million horses and mules were treated in veterinary hospitals in France. In round numbers, some eight million horses lost their lives in that war, plus countless mules and donkeys.

See also **WARRIOR**

JULIO McCAW
Horse who raced against Jesse Owens

Jesse Owens won four gold medals at the Berlin Olympics in 1936 – 100 metres, 200 metres, 4 x 100 metres relay and long jump – thereby undermining the Third Reich's theory of racial superiority.

But success on the track did not bring prosperity to Owens, and before the end of the year he was forced to take whatever work he could find. At one point he worked as a playground janitor, and later reflected: 'Sure, it bothered me. But at least it was an honest living. I had to eat.' He took part in novelty events, such as racing against trucks, cars and motorbikes, and he toured with the Harlem Globetrotters basketball team.

The first horse against whom Owens competed was a Thoroughbred named Julio McCaw. The Olympian had to run 100 yards; the horse (ridden by prominent Cuban jockey Pepe Cantino) 140 yards. Jesse Owens took full advantage to win narrowly, clocking 9.9 seconds. 'We'd have run right over him if the race had been a few yards longer,' Pepe Cantino graciously declared.

KANTHAKA
The Buddha's favourite horse

White in colour, like so many famous horses, Kanthaka enjoyed all manner of adventures with Prince Siddhartha, who became Gautama Buddha. Horse and prince teamed up to win competitions in archery and swordplay as well as riding. Kanthaka helped his master escape the royal palace and start a new life as an ascetic – following which the horse so missed Siddhartha that he died of a broken heart.

KHARTOUM
'Six hundred thousand dollars on four hooves'

The Godfather, directed by Francis Ford Coppola and released in 1972, was hailed as 'the greatest gangster picture ever made' by critic Pauline Kael. But horse lovers have a more ambivalent attitude towards the movie, thanks to one notorious scene.

Vito Corleone (the New York-based godfather, played by Marlon Brando) dispatches his aide Tom Hagen to Los Angeles to seek a favour from studio boss Jack Woltz.

Woltz invites Hagen to dinner at his sumptuously appointed estate, and over a pre-prandial drink offers to show him a thing of beauty. He takes Hagen to the stable block, where his pride and joy is stabled: a Thoroughbred stallion – 'six hundred thousand dollars on four hooves' – named Khartoum. 'I'm not going to race him, though,' Woltz tells Hagen. 'I'm going to put him out to stud.' (He has missed the point. Khartoum would have been even more valuable after a successful racing career.)

Over dinner, Woltz vehemently refuses Corleone's proposition brought by Hagen, and the evening ends in acrimony.

Then it is early morning, the dawn of another sun-drenched California day. The camera lingers over the swimming pool, then lifts into the bedroom where Jack Woltz is asleep. He stirs; starts waking up; gradually realises that there is something in the bed; scrambles round ever more frantically to find what it might be; then realises that whatever it is is covering him in blood.

The music reaches a crescendo. Woltz cringes back in horror, then screams . . . as he sees the severed head of Khartoum.

KINCSEM

Legendary nineteenth-century race-mare

Foaled in Hungary in 1874, Kincsem ('my treasure') was a

liver chestnut filly/mare who ran in fifty-four races over four seasons and was never beaten.

She was bred by Erno Blaskovich at the prestigious Kisber Stud, from where when she was a two-year-old – so the story goes – she was abducted, later to be found with a group of Romany travelling people. When Blaskovich asked the travellers why they had not stolen a better-looking horse – during her racing career she would be called 'as long as a boat' – one of the group replied: 'The other horses may be better-looking, but she was the best of the lot. She will be a champion.'

He wasn't wrong. As a two-year-old, Kincsem won ten races on ten different courses in Hungary, Austria and Germany. The following year she won seventeen more times, including Hungary's version of the Two Thousand Guineas, One Thousand Guineas, Oaks and St Leger, and the local Derby, plus the Emperor's Prize, in Vienna.

As a four-year-old she ventured even further afield: to Goodwood, where she easily won the Goodwood Cup as the outsider of three; and to France for the Grand Prix de Deauville. In 1878 she also won the Grosser Preis von Baden Baden, and returned to Baden Baden the following year for a repeat victory.

She died in 1887 – on her thirteenth birthday – but not before she had started to spread her outstanding ability to those who followed her. Her influence remains to this day, her modern descendants including among their number the 2012 Two Thousand Guineas and Derby winner, Camelot.

Whatever the Hungarian for 'tough as old boots' might be – that was Kincsem.

LA MARQUESA
One of two middle-aged lady travellers

Originally published in 1963, Penelope Chetwode's *Two Middle-Aged Ladies in Andalusia* is one of the most engaging travel books of the twentieth century – a sort of 'Tschiffely Lite'. (*See* **MANCHA AND GATO.**)

The equine half of the pairing is La Marquesa (the Marchioness), a bay mare with one white sock and, in the words of the human side, 'fat like a hunter at grass in midsummer'. She had been loaned to Chetwode by the Duke of Wellington, who had a farm in Spain and a suitable mount. 'She was twelve years old, more or less equivalent in horse age to my fifty-one years . . . So we were going exploring together – two middle-aged ladies in Andalusia.'

The Marquesa showed the occasional burst of mulishness,

but on the whole the relationship was harmonious – so much so that the book closes with Chetwode ruminating on the suggestion from St Thomas Aquinas that 'you cannot love a horse, as a horse cannot love you back'. Discuss.

LOCO
Pancho's horse

See **DIABLO**

LOTTERY
First winner of the Grand National – sort of

There is no disputing that this remarkable horse won the Liverpool Great Steeplechase in 1839. The issue is whether three previous runnings of an equivalent race made them prototype Grand Nationals or not. In any case, Lottery has always seemed the right sort of name to be associated with the great Aintree race. Like **ARKLE** after him, Lottery was so far ahead of his contemporaries that conditions were framed to produce a level playing field. In 1842 the entrance money for a race at Finchley made the stipulation: 'Lottery's entry fee £40, others £10.'

MAGNOLIA
George Washington's horse

See **NELSON**

MAKYBE DIVA
Only triple winner of the Melbourne Cup

Makybe Diva won the Melbourne Cup – 'The Race that Stops the Nation' in Australia, or least in the state of Victoria – in 2003, 2004 and 2005, thus becoming the first horse to win this historic race three times. She also won the prestigious Cox Plate in 2005.

Her name derives from the first two letters of the names of five of owner Tony Santic's employees: Maureen, Kylie, Belinda, Diane and Vanessa.

MALABAR

D.H. Lawrence's rocking-horse winner

'The Rocking-Horse Winner' by D.H. Lawrence was published in *Harper's Bazaar* in 1926, and first collected in *The Woman Who Rode Away and Other Stories* in 1928.

The plot centres around a family whose outward appearance proclaims them well-to-do and wealthy, whereas in reality they are maintaining a relentless struggle to finance their opulent lifestyle.

> And so the house came to be haunted by the unspoken phrase: *There must be more money! There must be more money!* The children could hear it all the time, though nobody said it aloud. They heard it at Christmas when the expensive and splendid toys filled the nursery. Behind the shining modern rocking-horse, behind the smart doll's house, a voice would start whispering: 'There *must* be more money! There *must* be more money!' And the children would stop playing, to listen for a moment. They would look into each other's eyes, to see if they had all heard. And each one saw in the eyes of the other two that they too had heard. 'There *must* be more money! There *must* be more money!'

Through an arrangement struck with Bassett the gardener and with the collaboration of his mother's brother, the young son Paul has been making bets on horse races, with spectacular success. But his mother Hester continues her spendthrift ways, and for Paul the imminent running of the Derby takes on an urgent significance. Try as he might, he cannot be sure about which horse will win – until two nights before the big race, his parents return from a party, and Hester, increasingly anxious, makes for Paul's bedroom:

She stood, with arrested muscles, outside his door listening. There was a strange, heavy, and yet not loud noise. Her heart stood still. It was a soundless noise, yet rushing and powerful. Something huge, in violent, hushed motion. What was it? What in God's name was it? She ought to know. She felt that she knew the noise. She knew what it was.

Yet she could not place it. She couldn't say what it was. And on and on it went, like a madness.

Softly, frozen with anxiety and fear, she turned the door-handle.

The room was dark. Yet in the space near the window, she heard and saw something plunging to and fro. She gazed in fear and amazement.

Then suddenly she switched on the light, and saw her son, in his green pyjamas, madly surging on the rocking horse. The blaze of light suddenly lit him up, as he urged the wooden horse, and lit her up, as she stood, blonde, in her dress of pale green and crystal, in the doorway.

'Paul!' she cried. 'Whatever are you doing?'

'It's Malabar!' he screamed in a powerful, strange voice. It's Malabar!'

His eyes blazed at her for one strange and senseless second, as he ceased urging his wooden horse. Then he fell with a crash to the ground, and she, all her tormented motherhood flooding upon her, rushed to gather him up.

But he was unconscious, and unconscious he remained, with some brain-fever. He talked and tossed, and his mother sat stonily by his side.

'Malabar! It's Malabar! Bassett, Bassett, I know. It's Malabar!'

So the child cried, trying to get up and urge the rocking-horse that gave him inspiration.

Malabar wins the Derby. 'You've made over seventy thousand pounds, you have,' Bassett tells the still delirious Paul, which makes total winnings of over eighty thousand. But Paul dies in the night:

> And even as he lay dead, his mother heard her brother's voice saying to her: 'My God, Hester, you're eighty-odd thousand to the good, and a poor devil of a son to the bad. But, poor devil, poor devil, he's best gone out of a life where he rides his rocking-horse to find a winner.'

The movie of *The Rocking-Horse Winner*, starring John Mills and Valerie Hobson, with John Howard Davies as Paul, was released in the UK in 1949.

MAN O' WAR
Fabled US racehorse

Man o' War won twenty of his twenty-one races in 1919 and 1920. He did not run in the 1920 Kentucky Derby, but among his victories were the Preakness Stakes and Belmont Stakes, and on his final racecourse appearance he beat the 1919 Triple Crown winner Sir Barton in a match race (i.e. a race with just two runners) in Canada.

On Man o' War's twenty-first birthday his doting owner Samuel Doyle Riddle sent the horse a cake bearing twenty-one candles. And when Man o' War died at the age of thirty in 1947 he was laid in state in his box, in a coffin lined with silk in the black and gold of Riddle's racing colours. His grave is under a massive bronze statue at the Kentucky Horse Park.

Will Harbut, the stallion man who looked after the horse for most of his stud career, famously described Man o' War as 'The mostest hoss that ever was.'

MANCHA and GATO
Tschiffely's horses

In the early 1920s, Aimé Tschiffely, a scion of an old Swiss family, was working as a teacher in Buenos Aires. His many extracurricular pursuits included football and boxing, but he reserved his greatest enthusiasm for clambering up into a gaucho saddle and galloping horses across the pampas. From this passion sprung a close interest in the Criollo – or Creole – breed, native to Argentina since its forebears had been brought to South America from Spain in 1535, and famous for toughness and durability.

Out on one of these gallops, Tschiffely concocted a madcap idea. He would test the hardiness of the Creole breed by riding the 10,000 miles from Buenos Aires to Washington DC. The resulting book, *Tschiffely's Ride*, became a classic of equine literature, whose contents are crisply summed up in the author's Foreword:

> I rode some 10,000 miles in two and a half years. From Argentina I came north, over cold, barren 16,000-foot ranges; then down into steamy jungles, across the Isthmus of Panama, up through Central America and Mexico, and so to the United States.

Tschiffely's companions for the ride were two horses considered physically and mentally well equipped for the adventure ahead.

Mancha (which means 'spotty') was described by Tschiffely as 'a red, with heavy irregular splashes of white; white face and stockings', and was eighteen years old when the trio departed from Buenos Aires.

Gato ('the cat') was sixteen: 'More or less of a coffee colour, a sort of a cross between a bay and a dun.'

(In the early editions of *Tschiffely's Ride* the ages of Mancha and Gato are given as sixteen and fourteen respectively, but Tschiffely later revised both figures.)

The beginning of the epic journey was not propitious. Both horses were fractious when being saddled – not a good augury for a trip of 10,000 miles, with Tschiffely riding Gato and Mancha serving as a reluctant pack-horse. Mancha, according to Tschiffely, 'had evidently decided that he would much prefer to go back to his stable, and I had to haul him along by main force'.

Eventually Mancha settled down, and they were on their way. From Buenos Aires they headed north, and by the time they reached the Bolivian Andes, man and horses had become the best of friends. They were, as the Gauchos put it, 'amadrinado'. According to Tschiffely, both Mancha and Gato were so relaxed in his company that they were happy to be turned out overnight, no matter what the conditions, and each morning they greeted him 'with a friendly nicker.'

They passed ancient stone monuments; skirted Lake Titicaca; encountered Inca ruins; crossed the Andes into Lima; struggled their way across desert ('For days the horses waded in deep, burning sand') and through dense jungle.

The months ticked by as they made their way from Peru into Ecuador. They swam across the crocodile-infested rivers of Colombia; then Panama . . . Costa Rica . . . Nicaragua . . . Honduras . . . El Salvador . . . Guatemala and Mexico. They entered the USA late in 1928 over the bridge into Laredo, then set off through Texas towards Washington DC.

They encountered all sorts of scrapes, obstacles and difficulties along the way, including bouts of illness in man and horses, but ironically, the worst incident occurred not on some remote mountain pass or deep in the forest, but close to their final destination.

To reduce the danger when riding on US roads, Gato had been left in St Louis, allowing Tschiffely and Mancha to proceed more rapidly towards Washington, and the horse seemed impervious to close shaves from speedy motorists. With DC almost in sight, Tschiffely was riding along the right-hand verge when a car appeared in the opposite carriageway.

The driver of the car steered across the road towards horse and rider, who were trapped between the highway and the roadside fence, with the inevitable result. The car rammed into Mancha and knocked him over, opening up a deep gash in his flank and left hind leg. Tschiffely was not badly injured. As for the perpetrator of this moronic prank, he did not stop to examine the damage he had wrought, but honked his horn and waved his hand as he roared off round the curve.

Mercifully, Mancha had not broken a bone, and after treatment to his wound and a suitable period of convalescence he was able to continue.

Upon reaching Washington in December 1928, Mancha was rewarded with a richly deserved bunch of carrots, and was soon reunited with Gato. The now famous twosome spent ten days at the International Horse Show in Madison Square Garden, New York City.

Mancha and Gato were then shipped back to Buenos Aires, where they were greeted as returning heroes. Offers to keep the pair in a public park were rejected in favour of returning them to the pampas, from which they had been taken to make their epic journey.

At the end of *Tschiffely's Ride*, the intrepid author writes:

> We decided that it would be kinder to allow them to spend the remaining years of their lives on a beautiful 'estancia' [estate] in the south of the province of Buenos Aires, and as I am writing these last lines I can see them galloping over the rolling plains until they disappear out of sight in the vastness of the pampas.

But that was not the last we hear of Mancha and Gato. *Tschiffely's Ride* was first published in January 1933 with the subtitle 'From Southern Cross to Pole Star', while *The Tale of Two Horses*, a children's book written by Tschiffely and published in 1934, tells their story in their own words. And in a piece datelined 'Chelsea, London, March 1951', Tschiffely provides a postscript to the story when he describes visiting Mancha and Gato some years after their return to Argentina:

> Although still some fifty yards away, I shouted, 'Mancha! Gato!' Immediately both turned round and stared at me, their heads held high, ears pricked up and nostrils dilated. I slowly approached the corral, and entered through the gate, the men watching with intense interest. I spoke to the animals, and they slowly came towards me. When I touched Mancha's broad forehead, both sniffed me all over . . . There could be no doubt they remembered me.

Gato died in 1944 at the age of thirty-five, and Mancha on Christmas Day 1947, at forty.

Tschiffely, who died in 1954, wrote several other books, including *Bridle Paths*, first published in 1936, in which he chronicles a ride through rural England on a mare named Violet.

MARENGO
Napoleon Bonaparte's favourite charger

Marengo was a light grey Arab stallion imported to France from Egypt in 1799 after the battle of Aboukir. Napoleon rode the seven-year-old at the battle of Marengo in 1800 and was so impressed by his mount's courage and nimbleness under fire – the emperor himself was wounded in the foot during that engagement – that he named him after the battle and went on to ride him at Austerlitz (after which battle another of Napoleon's chargers was named), Jena and Wagram.

Marengo also went on the expedition to Russia in 1812 – he unshipped the emperor on an icy road – and at the age of twenty-two in 1815 carried Napoleon at Waterloo, where the horse sustained an injury, the eighth time he had been wounded in action. After Napoleon had made his escape for Paris, the horse was abandoned in the battlefield stables, where he was captured by the British and taken to England by Lord Petre.

Marengo stood as a stallion at New Barnes, near Ely in Cambridgeshire, and died in 1831 at the considerable age of thirty-eight.

His skeleton is now in the National Army Museum in London.

MARSE ROBERT
Bit part in a famous movie

In the 1939 film of *Gone with the Wind*, Marse Robert is the name of the horse who pulls the buckboard driven by Rhett Butler during the burning of Atlanta. The name replicates a nickname for General Robert E. Lee: 'Marse' is the vernacular of 'Master'.

MIDNIGHT
Survived the fire when Grace did not

Since the radio soap opera *The Archers* was first broadcast in 1951, a steady procession of horses have trotted – or sounded as if they were trotting – along the highways and byways of the fictitious town of Ambridge, deep in the heart of Borsetshire.

Blossom and Boxer (the latter not to be confused with **BOXER** in *Animal Farm*) made a very early entrance to the programme as the last pair of working horses at Dan Archer's Brookfield Farm. When Dan bowed to the inevitable new technology in the guise of a tractor, Boxer was sold and Blossom put out to grass – though they came back in harness to pull the hay wagon bearing Letty Lawson-Hope's coffin in 1958.

By then the gelding with the most dramatic equine plot line of all had become a household name: Midnight.

Dan and Doris Archer bought the horse in 1952 as a twenty-first birthday present for their daughter Christine, who rode Midnight in point-to-point races. In September 1955 the Grey Gables stable yard where Midnight lived was engulfed by fire, and Grace, recently married wife of the Archers' son Phil, tried desperately to save the horse. She managed to get Midnight out, but as she went back in to rescue other horses a blazing wooden beam crashed down onto her head and knocked her out. She died in Phil's arms on the way to hospital.

This melodramatic incident has achieved mythic status in radio history, for Grace's demise just happened to occur on the day when the new commercial television channel first went on air. Was the BBC trying to steal ITV's thunder with a striking storyline? In the absence of hard evidence, the question has never been resolved one way or the other.

There has been nothing to match the demise of Grace for sheer drama, but an Archers plot has never been far from a horse. To name but a few: Grey Silk, a racehorse owned by Jack Woolley and Ralph Bellamy; Ambridge Flyer, Brian Aldridge's unimaginatively named point-to-point winner; Red Link, for whom in 1957 Paul and Christine engaged top (and real) showjumper Alan Oliver to assist in their attempt to compete in the Horse of the Year Show; Mister Jones, whose excellent jumping caught the eye of another leading showjumper, Ann Moore in 1974; Pensioner, at one point owned by Lilian Bellamy; Bartleby, Joe Grundy's trap-pulling pony; Cranford Crystal, who pulled the hay cart bearing the coffin at Nigel Pargetter's funeral.

Out of the saddle, the late Walter Gabriel had reason to be grateful to horses. On Derby Day 1983, the then eighty-six-year-old pulled off a hefty touch when another legend, jockey Lester Piggott, landed his ninth Derby on Teenoso to complete Walter's accumulator bet worth thousands of pounds.

MISS NESHAM
Multiple winner of England's oldest horse race

Run on the third Thursday of March and originally called the Kiplingcotes Plate, what is now known as the Kiplingcotes Derby is an informal race over four miles of open country in the East Yorkshire Wolds, about ten miles from Beverley and not far from Market Weighton.

And not just any old four miles of the East Yorkshire Wolds, as the *Racing Post* noted when covering the race in 2008:

> The race takes place over a course of about four miles, starting at an old stone post on the side of a tiny road near the village of Etton and proceeding along grass verges, across a stretch of tarmac, through a sea of mud, over the bridge which crosses the old railway line, alongside Ashslack Woods – the Tattenham Corner of the Kiplingcotes Derby – then across the A614 Market Weighton–Bridlington road (mercifully officially closed for the occasion) and along more grass verges to the winning post.

The race was first run way back in 1519, and 100 years later found greater financial stability when a group of local sportsmen, headed by the Earl of Burlington and including the splendidly named Cornelius Twizzleton esquire, came up with enough money to secure the race's future.

The rules are essentially as they were half a millennium ago.

The race is open to any horse or pony, though nowadays the race tends to be won by ex-racehorses running under assumed names.

By tradition the winner nets £50 and a trophy, while the

runner-up pockets every other entry fee, currently £4 a go. So it can be more profitable to finish second than first, a perversion of the usual sporting practice. *The Times* reported that after the 1972 running, Miss Cole-Walton's three-length lead cost her £24 (the first prize was £16, the second £40). 'But I don't really mind. It's much better to win.' That's the spirit!

Then there is the strange regulation regarding the weight to be carried by the rider. In a regular horse race, weights are allotted for each race, and jockeys may not ride in the race weighing less than stipulated. In the Kiplingcotes version the saddle is not weighed, and the rider must carry *more* than ten stone. If necessary, weights must add bulk to reach that mark. Riders shy of ten stone might stuff their pockets (or bumbags) with lead strips, and it is not unknown for a small person to make up the deficit with two or three bricks.

Another ancient rule was that, should the race not be run one year, it would cease for ever. When a recent running was abandoned on account of waterlogging, a doughty local farmer saddled his horse and walked over, thereby avoiding the extinction of what remains something of an oddity in horsy circles.

As for Miss Nesham, she has a prominent entry in the Kiplingcotes annals as the most prolific winner in the long history of the race, winning five years running between 1728 and 1732.

MISTER ED

Eponymous talking horse

The television comedy series *Mister Ed* first ran in the USA between early 1961 and September 1966 and was originally broadcast in the UK in 1964 and 1965. Architect Wilbur Post (played by Alan Young) moves with his wife Carol (Connie Hines) to a new home in Los Angeles, where in the barn they discover a palomino horse named Mister Ed, who has been left there by the previous owners. Ed has the unusual equine gift of being able to talk, though he will do so only to Wilbur – the first human he has seen fit to speak with – and cannot be heard by other humans.

The idea for the series came from Arthur Lubin, who in the 1950s had directed no fewer than seven movies about a talking donkey named Francis and had long harboured the notion of transferring the concept to the small screen. A notable guest appearance in *Mister Ed* came from seventy-year-old Mae West in March 1964.

MODESTINE
R.L. Stevenson's donkey

Robert Louis Stevenson (1850–1894) was one of the best-loved authors of the nineteenth century, some of whose stories – notably *Treasure Island, The Strange Case of Dr Jekyll and Mr Hyde* and *Kidnapped* – are still devoured today.

Pre-dating those books came *Travels with a Donkey in the Cevennes*, published in 1879, an account of a short ride undertaken the previous year – when, in need of a suitable conveyance, RLS addresses the need to acquire a beast of burden to accompany him on his journey:

> Now, a horse is a fine lady among animals, flighty, timid, delicate in eating, of tender health; he is too valuable and too restive to be left alone, so that you are chained to your

brute as to a fellow galley-slave; a dangerous road puts him out of his wits; in short, he's an uncertain and exacting ally, and adds thirty-fold to the troubles of the voyager. What I required was something cheap and small and handy, and of a stolid and peaceful temper; and all these requisites pointed to a donkey.

He visits Father Adam:

Father Adam had a cart, and to draw the cart a diminutive she-ass, not much bigger than a dog, the colour of a mouse, with a kindly and a determined under-jaw. There was something neat and high-bred, a quakerish elegance, about the rogue that hit my fancy on the spot.

Our first interview was in Monastier market-place. To prove her good temper, one child after another was set upon her back to ride, and one after another went head over heels into the air; until a want of confidence began to reign in youthful bosoms, and the experiment was discontinued from dearth of subjects. I was already backed by a deputation of my friends; but as if this were not enough, all the buyers and sellers came round and helped me in the bargain; and the ass and I and Father Adam were the centre of a hubbub for near half an hour. At length she passed into my service for the consideration of sixty-five francs and a glass of brandy.

The sack [luggage which he had bought before acquiring the donkey] had already cost eighty francs and two glasses of beer; so that Modestine, as I instantly baptized her, was upon all accounts the cheaper article. Indeed, that was as it should be; for she was only an appurtenance of my mattress, or self-acting bedstead on four castors.

The pair tour the Cevennes region for less than two weeks, from Monastier down to St Jean du Gard, and all too soon it is time to dispense with Modestine. She is sold for thirty-five francs, saddle and all, and only gradually does Stevenson realise how much he will miss her:

> For twelve days we had been fast companions; we had travelled upwards of a hundred and twenty miles, crossed several respectable ridges, and jogged along with our six legs by many a rocky and many a boggy by-road. After the first day, although sometimes I was hurt and distant in manner, I still kept my patience; and as for her, poor soul! she had come to regard me as a god. She loved to eat out of my hand. She was patient, elegant in form, the colour of an ideal mouse, and inimitably small. Her faults were those of her race and sex; her virtues were her own.

MOROCCO – BANKS'S HORSE
Elizabethan performer

Usually known as 'Banks's Horse' after his owner and handler William Banks (*fl.* 1591–1637), the horse named Morocco (sometimes *Marocco*) enjoyed a fame which few other horses in history can have matched. He was cited by such writers as Shakespeare, Jonson, Dekker, Nashe, Donne, Webster and Middleton, and over sixty allusions to this phenomenal creature have been traced in literature before 1675.

Banks himself seems to have come from Staffordshire, and he is first heard of as a performer in Shrewsbury in 1591 with 'a white horse which would do wonderful and strange things' – including counting, tapping out with his hoof the number of coins in a purse and identifying members of the audience by the colour of their coats. This white horse was probably a predecessor of the small gelding Morocco, who was usually described as bay and appears to have been foaled around 1589.

By the mid-1590s Morocco and Banks were one of the sensations of London – so sensational that it was widely held that some form of magic or witchcraft underpinned the act – and their performances, which usually consisted of a combination of counting and dancing, were alluded to in Shakespeare's *Love's Labour's Lost*, when Moth observes to Don Armado: 'How easy it is to put "years" to the word "three", and study three years in two words, the dancing horse will tell you.'

Morocco had many other accomplishments. He would kneel, lie down, play dead and even urinate – or, in equine parlance, stale – upon a command from Banks; he would bow at any mention of the queen, but would become very agitated and stubborn at any mention of the King of Spain. In 1595 he was celebrated in a book entitled *Maroccus Extaticus: or, Banks's Bay Horse in a Trance* which contains the only contemporary depiction of the horse: a crude woodcut shows Morocco standing on his hind legs with his forelegs raised and a long stick clenched in his mouth, and a pair of dice at his feet; Banks himself holds up another stick. (Morocco was often referred to as a 'curtal' – a horse with a docked tail – but in this woodcut has a tail of regulation length.)

Morocco's most spectacular performance took place early in February 1601 when Banks rode the horse up the narrow staircase all the way to the top of the steeple of St Paul's Cathedral. (The pre-Great Fire of London version of St Paul's had a steeple on top of a tower rather than a dome.) The cathedral was destroyed in the Great Fire of 1666, but it has been calculated that the ascent would have involved at least one thousand steps up a very hemmed-in spiral staircase – and the coming down would have been considerably more hazardous than the going up. Understandably there are many contemporary allusions to this feat. In the play *Satiromastix* by Dekker and Webster, written soon after the event, Horace has 'heard of the horse's walking a'th' top of Paul's'.

The ascent of St Paul's hugely increased the fame of horse and handler, and early in 1601 Morocco and Banks undertook a European tour. Jean de Montlyard, a spectator in Paris, gave a very detailed account of the act:

> [Morocco] fetched whatever anyone threw on the stage, and brought it back like a spaniel. He jumped and capered like a monkey. He stood on two legs, walked forward and backward, and then knelt, extending his hooves straight out in back of him. His master threw up a glove, commanded him to fetch it and carry it to whoever in the company wore (for example) spectacles. Morocco did so, approaching the wearer unerringly . . . His master covered his eyes with a cloak, then asked three of the audience for different coins of gold or silver. We saw him given a sol, a quarter écu, and an écu, then put them in a glove, remove the blindfold, and ask Morocco how many coins were in the glove. The horse struck the floor three times with his hoof to indicate three. Then his master asked how many were gold, and Morocco stamped only once, to say one . . . He commanded that he sneeze three times. He did it at once. That he laugh: he did likewise, showing his teeth and pricking his ears . . .

A magistrate in Paris, convinced that this was all the work of the Devil, had Banks imprisoned and Morocco impounded – until Banks demonstrated to the authorities how it was all done by subtle signs transmitted from him to the horse.

As with **CLEVER HANS** in a later period, the extraordinary abilities of Morocco can only have been the fruit of long period of training and of bonding between man and horse, a fact stressed by the greatest equine writer of the time, Gervase Markham. One chapter of his book *Cavelarice, or the English Horseman* (1607) describes 'how a horse may be taught to do any trick done by Banks his curtal' – and Markham clearly did not approve of making horses perform silly tricks which 'more properly do belong to dogs, apes, monkeys and baboons'.

There is no record of the act later than 1601, and the date of Morocco's death, like that of his birth, is not recorded. In 1608 Banks was paid by Prince Henry, son of James I, 'for teaching of a little nag to vault, by His Highness's command' and later for similar services by the Duke of Buckingham, and in his later years he opened a tavern. Nothing is heard of him after 1637, though a pamphlet published in 1662 referred to 'my fellow humourist Banks, the vintner in Cheapside, who taught his horse to dance, and shod him with silver'.

(The best account of Morocco and Banks is by Arthur Freeman in *Elizabeth's Misfits: Brief Lives of English Eccentrics, Exploiters, Rogues and Failures, 1580–1660*, published in 1978.)

MUFFIN THE MULE
Television puppet

Muffin the Mule became a television star in his own right in 1946, but the prototype mule had been produced in 1934 by puppet-maker Fred Tickner for the Hogarth Puppets. In his television incarnation Muffin's usual stamping ground was the top of the grand piano played by Annette Mills (sister of actor John); his strings were pulled from behind a screen by Ann Hogarth. The cast of *Muffin the Mule* gradually widened to include other alliteratively named characters such as Oswald the Ostrich, Louise the Lamb, Peter the Pup, Poppy the Parrot, Hubert the Hippo, Katy the Kangaroo, Monty the Monkey, Grace the Giraffe, Kirri the Kiwi, Willie the Worm and Zebbie the Zebra, as well as a pair of mice named Maurice and Doris.

Muffin made his final appearance with Annette Mills in 1955. She died a few days after that transmission, and Muffin's career did not long survive her: his final television appearance came on ITV in 1957, though a high-tech animated version reappeared on BBC Television in 2005.

Famously hard-working and resilient as well as famously stubborn, the mule was being used as a beast of burden over three thousand years ago, and has never managed to improve his image. A low point came with the description in the song 'Swinging on a Star', which was sung by Bing Crosby (and in the version by Big Dee Irwin that reached the Top Ten in Britain in 1963), which rolls out the mule clichés: he has long ears; kicks anything within range; brawny back; weak brain; stupid and stubborn. And children be warned: if you are disinclined to go to school, you may grow up to be a mule.

(In the 1970s Smirnoff vodka ran an extensive advertising campaign using the formula, 'I thought [*insert some innocent activity*] until I discovered Smirnoff.' An unofficial addition to the campaign, scrawled on various walls and hoardings around London, read: 'I thought Muffin the Mule was a sexual offence until I discovered Smirnoff.')

MY LITTLE PONY
Globally popular doll

My Little Pony started life as *My Pretty Pony* in 1981, making the switch to 'Little' the following year. Since then the doll has moved with the times and undergone several makeovers, coming in all sorts of forms in addition to the basic creature: books, video games, etc. Retail sales in recent years have regularly exceeded $1 billion annually.

Collectors talk in terms of 'Generations' of MLP material, and the current generation, located in a fantasy world called Equestria, was launched in 2010. Among the inhabitants of Equestria are Rainbow Dash, Twilight Sparkle, Pinkie Pet, Rarity, Applejack, Spike and Fluttershy.

NELSON
George Washington's favourite horse

George Washington (1732–1799), first president of the USA, was exceptionally accomplished in the saddle. Thomas Jefferson, Washington's secretary of state and third president, considered him 'the best horseman of his age, and the most graceful figure that could be seen on horseback', while George Custis, grandson of Washington's wife Martha, confirmed that view:

> Those who have seen Washington on horseback will admit that he was one of the most accomplished of cavaliers in the true sense and perfection of the character.
> He rode, as he did everything else, with ease, elegance, and with power. The vicious propensities of horses were

of no moment to this skilful and daring rider! He always said that he required but one good quality in a horse, to go along, and ridiculed the idea of its being even possible that he should be unhorsed, provided the animal kept on its legs. Indeed the perfect and sinewy frame of the admirable man gave him such a surpassing grip with his knees, that a horse might as soon disencumber itself of the saddle as of such a rider.

George Custis described Washington and his party pursuing his passion for hunting:

> The general usually rode in the chase a horse called Blueskin, of a dark iron-gray color, approaching to blue. This was a fine but fiery animal, and of great endurance in a long run . . .
>
> There were roads cut through the woods in various directions, by which aged and timid hunters and ladies could enjoy the exhilarating cry, without risk of life or limb; but Washington rode gaily up to his dogs, through all the difficulties and dangers of the ground on which he hunted, nor spared his generous steed, as the distended nostrils of Blueskin often would show. He was always in at the death, and yielded to no man the honour of the brush.

Magnolia, also spelled 'Magnolio' and judged 'a most beautiful creature' by a contemporary witness, was much in demand as a stallion, while Prescott was another notable horse of Washington's. George Custis again:

> Of the chargers the one usually rode by the chief [Washington] was named Prescott. He was a fine parade horse, purely white, and sixteen hands high. He was indifferent to the fire of artillery, the waving of banners,

and the clang of martial instruments, but had a very bad habit of dancing about on the approach of a carriage, a habit very annoying to his rider, who although a master of horsemanship, preferred to ride as quietly as possible . . .

A visitor to Washington's home in Mount Vernon in 1789 remarked:

Washington always preferred a white horse to any other, and this was so well known throughout the country that, when making a tour and approaching a town, the welcoming committee would have a steed of this colour ready for him to ride on his entry. He kept two of them in his own stables, both extremely beautiful animals, which he habitually rode in turn. One was named Prescott, the other Jackson . . .

It was on Prescott that Washington rode on his two presidential tours, to New England in 1789 and to the southern states two years later.

Yet for all the undoubted qualities of those equine heroes, Washington's own favourite mount was not another 'purely white', but a light sorrel-coloured horse who stood sixteen hands high, had a white face and legs, and had been described as 'a splendid charger' donated to Washington when he was in need of a new horse. The donor was Thomas Nelson, and the horse became Nelson.

During the revolutionary war, Washington is said to have preferred Nelson to Blueskin because he was less agitated by the sounds of battle, and it is significant that he rode Nelson on the day the British army under Lord Cornwallis surrendered to him at Yorktown.

It seems that Nelson was not ridden after the war. He

retired to join Blueskin in a life of leisure at Mansion House Farm, where he was often visited by the president. George Custis reported how, when seeing his Washington approach, 'the old war-horse would run, neighing, to the fence, proud to be caressed by the great master's hands'.

Nelson died in 1790 at the age of twenty-seven.

NIJINSKY
Triple Crown winner 1970

Lester Piggott, greatest of all jockeys on the Flat, rarely rhapsodised about the horses he rode. So the reaction to his first sighting of this famous racehorse is all the more remarkable:

> You couldn't help falling in love with Nijinsky as soon as you saw him. He was so big and imposing, with a real presence about him: in looks as in performance, he was simply outstanding.

Named after the late ballet dancer Vaslav Nijinsky and a son of the stallion Northern Dancer, Nijinsky the horse was bought by American industrialist Charles Engelhard and put into training in Ireland with Vincent O'Brien.

It soon transpired that Nijinsky could be difficult as well as brilliant. When he first arrived at O'Brien's he would not eat the local oats, and horse nuts had to be specially flown over from Canada. By the time the nuts arrived, the highly strung horse had consented to eat the oats after all.

Nijinsky won all his five races as a two-year-old in 1969 – notably the prestigious Dewhurst Stakes, when he was ridden by Piggott for the first time – and became a warm favourite for the 1970 Two Thousand Guineas and Derby. He opened his three-year-old account by beating Deep Run – later a phenomenally successful sire of jumpers – then cruised home in the Guineas, after which Piggott received a letter from the human Nijinsky's widow Romola, who had been at Newmarket for the big race:

> I was tremendously impressed with your magnificent winning of the Two Thousand Guineas race this afternoon on the beautiful horse Nijinsky, and I send you my congratulations. I ask of you now only one thing – please win the Derby for us!

Next came the Derby. On the eve of the big race he was stricken by a bout of colic and his participation was in doubt, but he recovered and, again ridden by Piggott, easily beat the French challenger Gyr. Invited to the royal box after the race to be presented to the Queen and Queen Mother, Engelhard realised that the braces on his morning suit had broken, but managed the remarkable feat of shaking royal hands while keeping the rest of his outfit intact. 'If I'd moved my arms,' he told O'Brien's wife Jacqueline later, 'my trousers would have fallen down!'

Nijinsky then won the Irish Derby (ridden by O'Brien's stable jockey in Ireland, Liam Ward) before sauntering home under Piggott to win the King George VI and Queen Elizabeth Stakes at Ascot with ridiculous ease.

No horse had won the English Triple Crown of Two Thousand Guineas, Derby and St Leger since Bahram in 1935, and Nijinsky's prospects did not look good when, during his preparation for the third leg, he contracted the skin disease American ringworm. The colt's principal autumn target was the Prix de l'Arc de Triomphe at Longchamp, and trainer O'Brien warned that a hard race in the St Leger, in addition to the effects of the ringworm, would make the Arc even more of a challenge. But Charles Engelhard knew that he was dying (he was addicted to Coca-Cola), and was desperate to achieve the Turf immortality of owning a Triple Crown winner. So the colt headed to Doncaster for the world's oldest Classic race.

Nijinsky duly won the St Leger to join the elite company of Triple Crown winners, and went on to Paris, where in the Arc he was controversially beaten by a head by Sassafras – with 'The Riders in the Stand' insisting that Piggott had left his challenge too late, and that they would have ridden him better.

It was his first defeat in twelve races.

In pursuit of a career-concluding victory, Nijinsky ran in the Champion Stakes at Newmarket. Even taking the Paris calamity into account, he was the most famous horse in the world, and the centre of attention. Confronted by a barrage of photographers, he boiled over, and had little nervous energy left for the race. He was beaten into second place by Lorenzaccio, a horse whom Nijinsky in his glorious prime would have picked up and carried.

He then retired to pursue a hugely profitable stud career in the USA, where his offspring included fellow Derby winners Golden Fleece, Shahrastani and (posthumously) Lammtarra.

A horse with an aura of sheer magic, Nijinsky died in 1992 at the age of twenty-five. A fine bronze of this great horse by Emma McDermott stands at the Curragh racecourse.

(For more on Lester Piggott, see THE CHASE.)

NUGGET
Horse in Equus

The play *Equus* by Peter Shaffer (1926–2016), which was first performed at the Old Vic Theatre in July 1973, with Alec McCowen playing the psychiatrist Martin Dysart, is a powerful and disturbing piece of work. The plot centres around the psychologically disturbed youth Alan Strang (Peter Firth in the original production), who has been blinding horses – among them Nugget. In trying to unravel what has been motivating Strang, Dysart is forced to confront his own demons, and the result is very uncomfortable viewing.

OCCIDENT
Participant in famous experiment

Occident was one of the four horses photographed at the gallop by Eadweard Muybridge, in order to prove the conviction of Leland Stanford (one-time governor of California and founder of Stanford University) that at one point in the stride, all four hooves are off the ground – and generations of equine artists had been wrong. Muybridge took pictures at one five-thousandth of a second with a series of twenty-four cameras, and duly captured the precise movements of the horse at full gallop.

OLD BILLY
Oldest horse ever?

Lancashire-bred Old Billy, a cross between Cleveland and

Eastern bloodlines, was reputedly foaled in 1760 and died sixty-two years later in 1822. He began his working life in the early 1760s with the Mersey and Irwell Navigation Company, with whom he was employed towing barges, and stayed with that company until he was retired. His skull is preserved in the Manchester Museum and his stuffed head in the Bedford Museum.

OLD BOB

Abraham Lincoln's horse

Abraham Lincoln (1809–1865) bought Old Bob when studying law in Illinois, and used him as a carriage horse (succeeding a horse named Old Buck in a similar role). When Lincoln became president in 1860 he sold the horse to a drayman's business in Springfield, but Old Bob was back with his one-time master following Lincoln's assassination, taking a prominent role in the funeral procession, immediately behind the hearse.

OLD KING

Influential albino stallion

As with other mammals, equine albinos have a congenital deficiency of colouring pigment. An albino horse has completely white hair, pink skin and – sometimes but not invariably – blue eyes. While albino is strictly a type rather than a breed, the American Albino, which was recognised as a breed with the founding of the American Albino Horse Club in Nebraska in 1937, supposedly traces back to a horse named Old King, who was by an Arab stallion out of a

Morgan mare, in the first decade of the twentieth century. In 1970 the American Albino Horse Club was renamed the American White Horse Club, and today the breed is called the American Creme.

PASCASAS

See INCITATUS

PEGASUS
The winged horse

As is the case with so many of the characters who populate classical mythology, there is no single version of the story of Pegasus. There tends to be consensus that his name derives from the Greek word for 'spring' (in the 'source of water' sense), and it was said that he was born 'at the springs of the ocean' – that is, in the far west. One mythological tradition has Pegasus springing from the Gorgon's neck after it had been slain and beheaded by Perseus, which would make him the son of Poseidon and the Gorgon.

Alternative versions of the narrative see the horse born of the earth, which has been fertilised by the Gorgon's blood.

And if you think that Greek mythology is confusing, consider this action-packed narrative.

Pegasus is absent from Helicon, but Bellerephon finds him drinking at Peirene, on the Acropolis of Corinth, and throws over his head a golden bridle, while some scholars insist that Athene gave Pegasus to Bellerephon already bridled. And so on and so on . . .

At the singing contest between the Pierides and the Muses, Mount Helicon expands with pleasure, at which Poseidon tells Pegasus to hit the mountain to regain its shape. Pegasus does so, and a spring starts gushing at the place where he had made contact – the Hippocrene, or Horse Spring. Later Pegasus is transformed into a constellation.

(For guidance through the minefield that is mythological literature, see Robert Graves, *The Greek Myths*, published 1955.)

PHANTOM
Zorro's horse

Phantom was the white stallion belonging to Zorro in the 1960s television series based on the creation of pulp writer Johnston McCulley. The other horse ridden by the masked vigilante was Tornado.

PHAR LAP
'The Red Terror'

Phar Lap – the name is Sinhalese for 'lightning' – inspired

manic devotion in the Australian racing world and beyond, and his memory lives on.

He was New Zealand-bred; sold as a yearling for 160 guineas; ran in fifty-one races between 1929 and 1932, winning thirty-seven, including the 1930 Melbourne Cup, in which he carried 9 stone 12 pounds, started at odds of 8/11, and won by three lengths. Later he moved to North America, and in March 1932 easily won the Agua Caliente Handicap in Mexico.

But a fortnight later he was dead. Rumour ran riot with the suggestion that he had been poisoned, but the true cause of his demise was never established.

Phar Lap had long since captured the communal heart of Australia, and his reputation was enhanced by his untimely demise. There were countless poems about the horse, and a song by Jack Lumsdaine, entitled 'Phar Lap – Farewell to You!':

Just a wonder horse,
Known on every course,
From Australia to the USA;
We're sad, old chap,
That your long last lap,
Has come and you've gone away.
Though there may be other champions,
Your memory will always be new,
Though your last race is run,
Why everyone says,
Phar Lap, farewell to you!

Nor were his remains allowed to rest in peace. Phar Lap was stuffed and put on display in the Melbourne Museum, from which he would be taken out once a year to participate in the pre-Melbourne Cup parade through the city.

The movie *Phar Lap*, released in 1983, sees a newspaper reporter asking the horse's trainer Harry Telford: 'Why is it, do you think, that there's been this incredible reaction to Phar Lap's death? After all, he was just a horse.'

'He wasn't just a horse,' Telford snaps back. 'He was the best.'

POOKA
Mythical Irish hobgoblin

'The Pooka', spelled in a variety of ways, is described thus in the *Oxford English Dictionary*: 'In Irish folklore – a malignant sprite or hobgoblin, *esp.* one which takes the form of an animal' – and that animal could be horse, cat, dog, hare, goat ... whatever. In *Fairy and Folk Tales of the Irish Peasantry* (1888), the poet W.B. Yeats calls the sprite 'essentially an animal spirit'.

Brian Boru, High King of Ireland, is the only person to have ridden the Pooka – that is, if you discount one of the drunkards taken by a horse-shaped hobgoblin on a manic night-time ride across the countryside, before being dumped on the ground back from where they had set off, and where the drunkard will eventually wake up.

But the life of the Pooka is not relentlessly destructive or mischievous, and some are a downright positive influence – especially for farmers.

PRINCE
The Durbeyfields' horse

The novel *Tess of the D'Urbervilles* by Thomas Hardy (1840–1928), first published in 1891, concerns the fortunes of the lowly Durbeyfield family – principally the wronged daughter

Tess – following the attempt to 'claim kin' with the more socially elevated D'Urbervilles.

The Durbeyfields' horse Prince has a brief but devastating appearance when, early one morning while it is still dark, he is harnessed to the waggon so that Tess and her brother Abraham can make a delivery of beehives to the local market.

[In the stable] the rickety little waggon was already laden, and the girl led out the horse Prince, only a degree less rickety than the vehicle.

The poor creature looked wonderingly round at the night, at the lantern, at their two figures as if he could not believe that at that hour, when every living thing was intended to be at shelter and at rest, he was called upon to go out and labour. They put a stock of candle-ends into the lantern, hung the latter to the off-side of the load, and directed the horse onward, walking at his shoulder at first during the uphill parts of the way, in order not to overload an animal of so little vigour.

As the trio continue towards town, Abraham grows drowsy, and as for the horse concerned: 'Prince required but slight attention, lacking energy for superfluous movements of any sort.'

Tess is dozing, when she is suddenly jolted awake:

A hollow groan, unlike anything she had ever heard in her life, came from the front, followed by a shout of 'Hoi, there!'

The lantern hanging at her waggon had gone out, but another was shining in her face – much brighter than her own had been. Something terrible had happened. The harness was entangled with an object which blocked the way.

In consternation Tess jumped down, and discovered the dreadful truth. The groan had proceeded from her father's poor horse Prince. The morning mail-cart, with its two noiseless wheels, speeding along those lanes like an arrow, as it always did, had driven into her slow and unlighted equipage. The pointed shaft of the cart had entered the breast of the unhappy Prince like a sword, and from the wound his life's blood was spouting in a stream, and falling with a hiss into the road.

In her despair Tess sprang forward and put her hand upon the hole, with the only result that she became splashed from face to skirt with the crimson drops. Then she stood helplessly looking on. Prince also stood firm and motionless as long as he could; till he suddenly sank down in a heap.

By this time the mail-cart man had joined her, and began dragging and unharnessing the hot form of Prince. But he was already dead.

Prince's horrible death sets off the chain of events which brings Tess to the scaffold.

PROMETEA
First cloned horse

See IDAHO GEM

QUADRIGA – THE HORSES OF ST MARK'S
'A very ancient and remarkable monument'

In statuary, a quadriga is a creation featuring four horses, and there is no finer example than the Horses of St Mark's in Venice.

These horses date from classical antiquity, and spent centuries in Constantinople before being removed to Venice, where they were located next to St Mark's Basilica. It was there that in 1608 the traveller Thomas Coryate was stopped in his tracks by the sight of 'a very ancient and remarkable monument, four goodly brass horses made of Corinthian metal, and fully as great as the life'.

The account in *Coryate's Crudities* (1611) continues:

These horses are advanced on certain curious and beautiful

pillars, to the end they may be the more conspicuous and eminent to be seen of every person. Of their forefeet there is but one set on a pillar, and that is of porphyry marble; the other foot he holdeth up very bravely in his pride which maketh an excellent shew.

In 1798 the horses were appropriated by Napoleon, who had them carted off to Paris – only to return to Venice in 1815. They remained in position at St Mark's Basilica until the early 1980s, when they were moved inside the cathedral, replaced outside by replica copies.

(A good up-to-date account is Charles Freeman's *The Horses of St Mark's: A Story of Triumph in Byzantium, Paris and Venice*, 2010.)

QUAGGA
Relative of the horse

In 1834 the naturalist Thomas Pringle described his encounter with an unusual, zebra-like animal in southern Africa: 'The poor quagga . . . is a timid animal with a gait and figure much resembling those of an ass.'

In 1859, in *The Origin of Species by Means of Natural Selection*, Charles Darwin had been considering variations in animal markings, and noted: 'The Quagga, though so plainly barred like a zebra over the body, is without bars on the legs.'

And in 2014, in a *Guardian* article about the Grant Museum of Zoology at University College, London, being proud owners of a three-legged female quagga – the missing limb had gone out on loan and had never been returned – Maev Kennedy observed: 'Quaggas look like zebras which had forgotten to put on their pyjama trousers, half stripey, half plain brown.'

The quagga – 'Equus or Hippotigris Quagga', to be formal – was closely related to the zebra and to the ass, and had attracted attention from naturalists on account of that eccentric marking. But the attention could not arrest the gradual decline in numbers. According to the journal *Nature*, the last quagga died in the Amsterdam zoo in the 1880s – 'but it is thought that this one had outlived by several years the wild quagga in South Africa'.

Maev Kennedy again: 'Once plentiful on the South African plains, quaggas were hunted both for their unusual skins and by stock keepers to reduce competition for food. London Zoo once had one, but it was only realised that the animal was extinct when the quagga in Amsterdam died on 12 August 1883. The zoo sent out hunters to bring back another one and found there were none left.'

QUIXALL CROSSETT
'Life: that is what horses are good at'

In the annals of losing, Quixall Crossett was right up there with the best. Between February 1990 and November 2001 he ran in 104 races and lost them all. He was beaten in eighty-four steeplechases and eighteen hurdles, plus a single National Hunt Flat Race ('bumper') and one point-to-point, and he netted £8,502 in place money.

His name derives from two elements: after Albert Quixall, the dashing footballer whose move from Sheffield Wednesday to Manchester United in 1958 for £45,000 was then a British transfer record; and after High Crossett, the remote North

Yorkshire farm from which the horse's trainer Ted Caine operated.

Quixall Crossett had one very close call. In a steeplechase at Wetherby in May 1998 – ridden by amateur Jim Crowley, later champion jockey on the Flat – he produced an unwonted turn of foot towards the end of the race and was fast catching odds-on favourite Toskano. But the post came just in time, and Quixall Crossett's unblemished record remained intact.

Quixall Crossett had a fan club as well as his own website (very high-tech at the time), and his one hundredth race (and one hundredth defeat) attracted widespread press attention.

Some racing professionals reacted snootily to what they saw as a perverse celebration of defeat, but behind the perennial loser was a poignant story.

When Quixall Crossett was a young horse, the Caines's son Malcolm had been killed in a farm accident and, as Ted Caine observed to *Times* journalist Simon Barnes, 'It was Quixall that kept us going, really.' Barnes's wistful piece on the Caines, written in March 1999 and reprinted in his book *On Horseback* (2000), stresses the therapeutic power of horses: 'It becomes clear that Quixall Crossett has seen the Caines through a period of the most unspeakable grief. Life: that is what horses are good at. That is what horses give.'

Quixall Crossett died in 2006 at the age of twenty-one.

RED RUM
Grand National treasure

With Red Rum, it is well nigh impossible to avoid one particular cliché: that his is a rags-to-riches story.

He was an unfashionably bred horse from the boondocks who went through the hands of a variety of handlers before ending up with an obscure trainer who divided his time between his racing operation and selling second-hand cars in Southport, near Liverpool. The training yard was tucked away behind the car showroom, and for exercise the horses walked down the busy streets to gallop on the beach.

Foaled in Ireland in 1965, Red Rum was sold as a yearling at public auction for a mere four hundred guineas, to jockey/trainer Tim Molony, and first raced as a two-year-old in a humble selling plate (£133 to the winning owner) in April 1967.

He dead-heated with a horse named Curlicue, then won twice more on the Flat, and was briefly in the charge of Tommy Stack, who features later in the Red Rum story. In all, Red Rum went through five different trainers during his racing life.

By the early 1970s he was plagued by the foot disease pedal osteitis, and in August 1972 was sold at auction again – this time for six thousand guineas – to trainer-cum-car-dealer Donald 'Ginger' McCain.

Whether McCain was a training genius, or whether Red Rum's foot problem was eased by all that walking and galloping along Southport beach – the probable answer is a combination of the two – the horse started to show a marked improvement in his form, and by spring 1973 he was one of the most promising young steeplechasers in the north of England. Indeed, he was so promising that he started joint favourite for that year's Grand National at Aintree, bracketed in the betting market with the top weight, the popular Australian chaser Crisp – a horse of undoubted class but dubious stamina.

Crisp turned in the most memorable single performance in Grand National history, jumping flamboyantly and maintaining such a relentless gallop that by Becher's Brook on the second circuit he was leading by a mammoth margin – and not stopping. As Crisp, who was conceding 23 pounds to his rival, approached the last two fences he was still way ahead of Rummy in second place, but jockey Brian Fletcher was ever so gradually cutting down the deficit, and Crisp was getting very tired. On the run-in between the last fence and the winning post, Crisp was running on fumes. Just short of the line Red Rum got his nose in front, and won by three-quarters of a length.

A year later Crisp was sidelined by injury, and Red Rum took full advantage to beat L'Escargot easily and become the first back-to-back Grand National winner for nearly forty years.

Red Rum was second to L'Escargot in 1975 and to Rag Trade in 1976, so in 1977 lined up with the remarkable record of four Grand National runs yielding two wins and two seconds.

His one-time trainer Tommy Stack was now his regular jockey, and in spite of Rummy's advancing years – he was by this time twelve years old – and top weight yet again, he scampered sure-footedly round Aintree to become the first horse ever to land the Grand National three times. This feat afforded him the opportunity of appearing on the BBC Television annual jamboree, the *Sports Personality of the Year* awards programme, where he stole the limelight from Tommy Stack. ('He's much cleverer than I am,' said the jockey.)

A training setback scuppered his chance of a run in the 1978 National, and Red Rum retired from the track. But his was not a quiet retirement, and he soon established himself as the first modern celebrity equine. He made personal appearances – mainly opening new betting shops – and promoted a limited-edition sports jacket which incorporated hairs from his tail.

More permanent are Red Rum statues at Aintree racecourse and at Ayr, where he won the Scottish Grand National in 1974, and like other famous horses he was the subject of a song. (*See* **STEWBALL**.)

Red Rum died at the age of thirty in October 1995, and is buried by the winning post at Aintree.

ROB ROY
Winston Churchill's first pony

See **COLONIST II**

ROCINANTE
Don Quixote's steed

Don Quixote of La Mancha by Miguel de Cervantes, the perennially popular chronicle of the exploits of the delusional 'knight', was first published in two parts in 1605 and 1615, with some editions spelling 'Rozinante' rather than 'Rocinante'.

In the first chapter, Don Quixote is busy acquiring the requisites for knighthood, in which the choice of horse is crucial. He lights upon a nag who is all skin and bone – but to Quixote's eye, well superior to **BUCEPHALAS** or **BAVIECA**.

He spends four days choosing the horse's name – 'for, he reflected', according to one translation:

> It was not right that a horse belonging to a knight so
> famous, and one with such merits of his own, should be
> without some distinctive name, and he strove to adapt
> it so as to indicate what he had been before belonging
> to a knight-errant, and what he then was; for it was
> only reasonable that, his master taking a new character,
> he should take a new name, and that it should be a
> distinguished and full-sounding one, befitting the new
> order and calling he was about to follow. And so, after
> having composed, struck out, rejected, added to, unmade,
> and remade a multitude of names out of his memory and
> fancy, he decided upon calling him Rocinante, a name,
> to his thinking, lofty, sonorous, and significant of his

condition as a hack before he became what he now was, the first and foremost of all the hacks in the world.

The mount of Don Quixote's 'squire' Sancho Panza is a donkey named Dapple.

ROLAND
Bringer of the good news – whatever it was

The poem 'How They Brought the Good News from Ghent to Aix' was first published in the 1845 collection *Dramatic Romances and Lyrics* by Robert Browning (1812–1889), and ever since has been regarded as one of the best-loved verses in the English language.

Reasons for that affection are not hard to find. The galloping rhythm of the metre and the atmosphere which suffuses every line are an irresistible combination. And there is no disputing who is the poem's true hero: Roland, 'my horse without peer'.

In April 1889 – not long before he died – Browning was at a dinner party at which each of the guests was asked to make a recording on a new-fangled device called a phonograph.

Initially reluctant, Browning started reciting 'Ghent to Aix' into the machine, but got no further than the first verse before forgetting the words. 'I'm terribly sorry,' he is heard apologising above the crackle, 'but I can't remember my own verses.' Now accessible through the British Library Sound Archive, this is thought to be the only recording of Browning's voice.

'How They Brought the Good News from Ghent to Aix' is not a poem to be perused in a quiet corner. Rather it should be read aloud – if your fellow rail-travellers look bewildered, so be it – and in full:

I sprang to the stirrup, and Joris, and he;
I galloped, Dirck galloped, we galloped all three;
'Good speed!' cried the watch as the gate-bolts undrew;
'Speed!' echoed the wall to us galloping through
Behind shut the postern the lights sank to rest
And into the midnight we galloped abreast.

Not a word to each other; we kept the great pace
Neck by neck, stride by stride, never changing our place;
I turned in my saddle and made its girths tight,
Then shortened each stirrup, and set the pique right,
Rebuckled the cheek-strap, chained slacker the bit,
Nor galloped less steadily Roland a whit.

'Twas moonset at starting, but while we drew near
Lokeren, the cocks crew and twilight dawned clear;
At Boom, a great yellow star came out to see;
At Düffield 'twas morning as plain as could be;
And from Mecheln church-steeple we heard the half-chime,
So Joris broke silence with, 'Yet there is time!'

At Aerschot, up leaped of a sudden the sun,
And against him the cattle stood black every one,
To stare thro' the mist at us galloping past,
And I saw my stout galloper Roland at last,
With resolute shoulders, each butting away
The haze, as some bluff river headline its spray.

And his low head and crest, just one sharp ear bent back
For my voice, and the other pricked out on his track;
And one eye's black intelligence, – ever that glance

O'er its white edge at me, his own master, askance!
And the thick heavy spume-flakes which aye and anon
His fierce lips shook upwards in galloping on.

By Hasselt, Dirck groaned; and cried Joris, 'Stay spur!
Your Roos galloped bravely, the fault's not in her,
We'll remember at Aix – for one heard the quick wheeze
Of her chest, saw the stretched neck and staggering knees,
And sunk tail, and horrible heave of the flank,
As down on her haunches she shuddered and sank.

So we were left galloping, Joris and I,
Past Looz and past Tongres, no cloud in the sky;
The broad sun above laughed a pitiless laugh,
'Neath our feet broke the brittle bright stubble like chaff;
Till over by Dalhem a dome-spire sprang white
And 'Gallop,' gasped Joris, 'for Aix is in sight!'

'How they'll greet us!' – and all in a moment his roan
Rolled neck and croup over, lay dead as a stone;
And there was my Roland to bear the whole weight
Of the news which alone could save Aix from her fate,
With his nostrils like pits full of blood to the brim,
And with circles of red for his eye-sockets' rim.

Then I cast loose my buffcoat, each holster let fall,
Shook off both my jack-boots, let go belt and all,
Stood up in the stirrup, leaned, patted his ear,
Called my Roland his pet-name, my horse without peer;
Clapped my hands, laughed and sang, any noise, bad or good,
Till at length into Aix Roland galloped and stood.

> *And all I remember is, friends flocking round*
> *As I sat with his head 'twixt my knees on the ground,*
> *And no voice but was praising this Roland of mine,*
> *As I poured down his throat our last measure of wine,*
> *Which (the burgesses voted by common consent)*
> *Was no more his due who brought good news from Ghent.*

After all that fuss, what exactly *was* 'the good news'? Nobody knows.

RONALD

Earl of Cardigan's mount at the Charge of the Light Brigade

Someone had blundered. Near Balaclava on the morning of 25 October 1854, at the height of the Crimean War, James Thomas Brudenell, 7th Earl of Cardigan, mounted his feisty chestnut charger Ronald, and led his Light Brigade towards the valley where, he had been told by his commanders, Russian positions on the side of the valley were there for the taking. What he had not been told was that there were enemy emplacements on the other side of the valley as well.

William Howard Russell of *The Times* graphically reported what happened to the Light Brigade:

> As they passed towards the front, the Russians opened on them from the guns in the redoubts on the right, with volleys of musketry and rifles.
>
> They swept proudly past, glittering in the morning sun in all the pride and splendour of war. We could hardly believe the evidence of our senses! Surely that handful of men were not going to charge an army in position? Alas! it was but too

true – their desperate valour knew no bounds, and far indeed was it removed from its so-called better part, discretion.

They advanced in two lines, quickening their pace as they closed towards the enemy. A more fearful spectacle was never witnessed than by those who, without the power to aid, beheld their heroic countrymen rushing to the arms of death.

At the distance of 1,200 yards the whole line of the enemy belched forth, from thirty iron mouths, a flood of smoke and flame, through which hissed the deadly balls. Their flight was marked by instant gaps in our ranks, by dead men and horses, by steeds flying wounded or riderless across the plain.

The first line was broken – it was joined by the second; they never halted or checked their speed an instant. With diminished ranks, thinned by those thirty guns, which the Russians had laid with the most deadly accuracy, with a halo of flashing steel above their heads, and with a cheer which was many a noble fellow's death cry they flew into the smoke of the batteries; but ere they were lost from view, the plain was strewed with their bodies and with the carcasses of horses.

There has long been dispute about the exact tally of dead and wounded, human and equine. One source calculated that 673 horsemen began the charge, of whom 113 were killed and 134 wounded, with 474 horses lost in the field of battle and forty-two wounded. Another source claimed that 362 horses were lost. Whatever the figures, there is no disputing the carnage that day; carnage that stirred Alfred, Lord Tennyson, then Poet Laureate, to now very familiar verse:

Cannon to right of them,
Cannon to left of them,
Cannon behind them
Volley'd and thunder'd;
Storm'd at with shot and shell,
While horse and hero fell,
They that had fought so well
Came thro' the jaws of Death,
Back from the mouth of Hell,
All that was left of them,
Left of six hundred.

Ronald was retired to the Cardigan country estate, Deene Park in Northamptonshire, where he lived a placid retirement, disturbed only by human admirers who wanted a souvenir in the form of a few of his tail hairs.

In 1868 this leisurely life was interrupted by the death of the earl, and Ronald was deployed to lead the funeral procession. The story goes that his attendants were so worried that this high-mettled horse would boil over while carrying out his ceremonial duties that a large dose of laudanum was administered to him, causing him to keel over and enter a deep sleep – from which he emerged just in time to attend the funeral, behaving perfectly.

Ronald died in 1872 but is still at Deene Park – to be precise, his head is still there, stuffed and mounted in a glass case, along with other relics of the famous horse.

ROSSA PRINCE
(and MISTER CHIPPENDALE)
Linked in infamy

A walkover is a 'race' in which, for whatever reason, there is only one runner. The standard procedure is that the rider of that runner weighs out at the scales, and after a brief saunter up the course turns and canters back past the winning post – and, crucially, past the judge in his or her booth. The rider then weighs in, and the result is confirmed. What could be more straightforward?

So big it up for Rossa Prince, a horse with a highly unusual claim to fame. At a point-to-point meeting at Tweseldown, Hampshire, in May 1990 he got loose while being tacked up, and was seen heading over the horizon when he should have been going through the pre-'race' motions. He was not apprehended soon enough to enter the paddock within the regulation time and was disqualified from the race, but he secured his place in the annals of point-to-point racing as the Horse Who Lost a Walkover.

This was a remarkable achievement by Rossa Prince, but the episode is not unique. At Southwell, Nottinghamshire, in April 1994 a point-to-pointer named Mister Chippendale lost a walkover when his jockey, having steered his horse past the winning post, failed to weigh in. The jockey had been shopped to the stewards by an observant racegoer described in the point-to-point form book as 'a disapproving old busybody'.

SCOT
The Reeve's horse

The only named horse in the 'General Prologue' to Geoffrey Chaucer's *Canterbury Tales* is the 'pomely [dappled] grey' called Scot, mount of the Reeve. (A reeve was a sort of estate manager.)

Horses ridden by the Reeve's companions on the road to Canterbury form a diverse bunch who reflect the status of their riders. For instance, according to the historian Barbara Tuchman in *A Distant Mirror*:

> The horse was the seat of the noble, the mount that lifted
> him above other men. In every language except English, the
> word for knight – *chevalier* in French – meant the man on
> horseback. 'A brave man mounted on a good horse,' it was

acknowledged, 'can do more in an hour of fighting than ten or maybe one hundred could do afoot.' The *destrier* or war-horse was bred to be 'strong, fiery, swift, and faithful' and ridden only in combat. En route the knight rode his palfrey, high-bred but of quieter disposition, while his squire led the *destrier* at his right hand – hence its name, from *dexter*. In fulfilling military service, horse and knight were considered inseparable; without a mount the knight was a mere man . . . For a knight to ride in a carriage was against the principles of chivalry and he never under any circumstances rode a mare.

In the 'General Prologue' – and in modern translation – the Knight's 'horses were good', while the Squire's equestrian skills are likewise praised: 'He was a good rider and sat his horse well.' The Monk 'kept plenty of fine horses in his stable, and when he went out riding people could hear the bells on his bridle jingling in the whistling wind . . . The horse he rode was as brown as a berry.' (In the original Middle English, the Monk's horse was described thus: 'His palfrey was as broun as is a berye.' A palfrey was a light-framed riding horse.)

The horse ridden by the ascetic Clerk of Oxford 'was as lean as a rake', while the scholar himself 'was no fatter, but looked both melancholy and hollow-cheeked'. The Shipman rode on a 'rouncy' – a carthorse, or a notably strong and powerful mount.

As for the Wife of Bath, 'She rode comfortably upon an ambling horse.' (The equine gait known as ambling has the horse lifting both its feet on one side simultaneously, rendering the ambler especially well suited for riding long distances.)

In addition, although the Merchant's horse is not described, his riding style is: he rode 'seated on a high saddle'.

SCOTT'S PONIES
Unsung heroes of Scott expedition in the Antarctic

On 1 December 1911 Robert Falcon Scott wrote in his diary:

> Under the forecastle fifteen ponies side by side, seven one
> side, eight the other, heads together and groom between –
> swaying continually to the plunging, irregular motion.
>
> One takes a look through a hole in the bulkhead and
> sees a row of heads with sad, patient eyes come swinging
> up together from the starboard side, whilst those on the
> port swing back; then up come the port heads, whilst the
> starboard recede. It seems a terrible ordeal for these poor
> beasts to stand this day after day for weeks together, and
> indeed though they continue to feed well the strain quickly
> drags down their weight and condition; but nevertheless
> the trial cannot be gauged from human standards. There
> are horses which never lie down, and all horses can sleep
> standing; anatomically they possess a ligament in each leg
> which takes their weight without strain. Even our poor
> animals will get rest and sleep in spite of the violent motion.

And on 7 January 1912:

> The ponies are working well now, but beginning to give some
> excitement. On the whole they are fairly quiet beasts, but they
> get restive with their loads, mainly but indirectly owing to
> the smoothness of the ice. They know perfectly well that the
> swingle trees and traces are hanging about their hocks and hate
> it. (I imagine it gives them the nervous feeling that they are
> going to be carried off their feet.) This makes it hard to start
> them, and when going they seem to appreciate the fact that
> the sledges will overrun them should they hesitate or stop. The

result is that they are constantly fretful, and the more nervous ones tend to become refractory and unmanageable.

Oates [Captain Oates, who before long would be stepping outside, possibly for some time] is splendid with them – I do not know what we should do without him.

SCOUT
Tonto's horse in The Lone Ranger

See **SILVER**

SECRETARIAT
A force of nature

Secretariat landed the US Triple Crown – Kentucky Derby, Preakness and Belmont Stakes – in 1973. Of the three, the most spectacular performance came in the final leg at Belmont Park, New York, which Secretariat won by an astonishing thirty-one lengths in record time. This effortlessly smooth performance occasioned journalist Charlie Hatton to pen one of the great racing quotations: 'He could not have moved faster if he had fallen off the grandstand roof.'

The movie *Secretariat*, starring Diane Lane and John Malkovich, was released in 2010.

SEFTON
Survivor of Hyde Park bomb

Irish-bred, like most Household Cavalry horses, Sefton was a cross between a Thoroughbred stallion and an Irish Draught mare. He was foaled in County Waterford in 1963, and as a four-year-old was sold to the British army, arriving in 1967 at the Wellington Barracks in London, where he acquired the nickname 'Sharky' on account of his readiness to bite.

On the morning of 20 July 1982 a detachment of the Blues and Royals including Sefton (ridden by Michael Pedersen) was trotting along South Carriage Road, Hyde Park, en route to duties in Horseguards' Parade in Whitehall, when a nail bomb concealed in a car they were passing exploded. Two Guardsmen were killed by the blast, and seventeen bystanders badly injured, while seven of the Blues and Royals horses were either killed instantly or rapidly put down.

Two hours later, not far away in Regent's Park, another bomb exploded underneath a bandstand, killing seven soldiers. Subsequently the IRA claimed responsibility for both atrocities.

Sefton survived, but sustained terrible injuries, including a severed jugular vein, and he underwent lengthy surgery. While convalescing, he received a constant supply of get-well cards and tubes of mints, and over £620,000 was raised in recognition. These donations went towards construction of a new surgical wing at the Royal Veterinary College – named the Sefton Surgical Wing – while the horse himself, who had eventually returned to his duties, appeared at the Horse of the Year show.

He retired from the Household Cavalry in 1984 and died in 1993.

SHADOWFAX

Totemic horse in The Lord of the Rings

The Lord of the Rings by J.R.R. Tolkien, published in three volumes in 1954 and 1955, features many horses, some of which prove more useful to the narrative thrust of this monumental work than others.

But there is no disputing the importance of Shadowfax. A descendant of Felarof, he is the greatest horse of Middle-earth – said to be capable of understanding human speech, and to be able to run faster than the wind. His coat is described as silvery-grey by daylight and almost invisible by night.

Shadowfax was totally undomesticated until catching the attention of Gandalf, who tamed the horse and rode him into battle throughout the War of the Ring. At the end of the Third Age he passed over the sea with Gandalf.

Other prominent equine characters in *The Lord of the Rings* include the speedy Arod; the pony Bill, alliteratively purchased in Bree by Barliman Butterbur, inn-keeper of the Prancing Pony, and later a pack-animal; Fatty Lumpkin; the aforementioned Felarof; and Snowmane, who died in battle (struck by a dart from the Witch King) and was buried where he had fallen, in a mound named 'Snowmane's Howe'.

SEABISCUIT
Granite-tough American racehorse of the 1930s and 1940s

Seabiscuit won thirty-three of his eighty-nine races and earned over US$400,000. He won many big races, most famously the Pimlico Special match race against the equine aristocrat War Admiral in November 1938. The scrapper, ridden by George 'Ice Man' Woolf, beat the toff by four lengths.

Seabiscuit was the subject of an acclaimed book by Laura Hillenbrand, which won the William Hill Sports Book of the

Year in 2001. The sponsors called the book 'a riveting tale of grit, grace, luck and an underdog's stubborn determination to win against all odds' – which was in essence the story of Seabiscuit's life. That book formed the basis for the 2003 movie.

SHERGAR
Famous racehorse who met a terrible end

Shergar, owned and bred by the Aga Khan and trained in Newmarket by Michael Stoute, was a brilliant racehorse. In 1981 the dark bay with the large white blaze on his face won the Derby by ten lengths under young Walter Swinburn, a record margin in the long history of that race. Ridden by Lester Piggott, Shergar then won the Irish Derby at the Curragh in a hack canter, and treated older rivals with similar contempt in the King George VI and Queen Elizabeth Stakes at Ascot. But he was retired after finishing fourth in the St Leger, and sent to the Aga Khan's Ballymany Stud in County Kildare. Such was the delight at having so great a horse stand as a stallion in Ireland that Shergar was paraded up the main street of Newbridge, near the stud, surrounded by cheering crowds.

Shergar's first season as a stallion in 1982 passed without incident, and his future looked secure.

That all changed on the evening of 8 February 1983 – a week before the 'covering season' was about to resume – when Shergar was abducted from the stud. His captors drove into the main entrance, threatened stud groom Jim Fitzgerald at gunpoint and forced him to load the horse into his horsebox. Fitzgerald was ejected from the horsebox in a remote area of countryside, and the horse vanished into thin air.

Shergar was never heard of again, but his disappearance

set off a small industry of books, documentaries, a ludicrous movie and a fresh spring in the step of hoaxers, clairvoyants and water-diviners. (In dubious taste was a Jak cartoon in the *Standard*, in which a horse pulling the milk-float is careering out of frame in a flurry of broken milk bottles, while two ladies – one holding a newspaper whose headline reads, 'Where is Shergar?' – watch on. One lady is saying to the other: 'Bejesus, Mary! Did you ever see Murphy do O'Connell Street in 35 seconds before?')

Into the void left by an almost complete lack of evidence with regard to Shergar's fate poured a range of theories, most of them suggesting the IRA as the villains, some involving Colonel Gadafy, the New Orleans mafia or a vengeful bloodstock dealer wronged by the Aga Khan. Not to mention the story that Shergar had swum to a boat lurking off the Waterford coast, from where he was taken to Saudi Arabia to cover mares for a mega-rich potentate.

In 1991 the *Sun* located Shergar in a field in the Channel Islands, and a special mention goes to the *Sunday Sport*, who reported a definite sighting of the horse being ridden by Lord Lucan.

Ransom demands from his kidnappers – assumed to be the IRA on a fund-raising mission – went unheeded by the syndicate of breeders who now owned the horse. Journalists were sent off on 'in search of Shergar' stories, all of which proved fruitless, and very soon the trail went cold. In June 1983 Lloyds of London, insurers of Shergar, paid out £7 million to the syndicate members – a formal assertion that the horse was dead.

(*In Search of Shergar* by Colin Turner – a journalist close to the story – was published in 1984.)

SHOSCOMBE PRINCE
The final Sherlock Holmes story

'Shoscombe Old Place' was the last Sherlock Holmes story, and the second which revolved around horse racing, following the far superior **SILVER BLAZE**.

First published in 1927 and collected in *The Case-Book of Sherlock Holmes*, the story tells how Sir Robert Norberton is in an extreme financial pickle through reckless gambling, and can be spared ruin only if his horse Shoscombe Prince wins the Derby. 'He thinks of nothing but the horse and the race,' trainer John Mason tells Holmes. 'His whole life is on it.'

The plot of 'Shoscombe Old Place' is too thin to be recounted here. 'Shoscombe Prince did win the Derby,' concluded Watson. 'The sporting owner did net eighty thousand pounds in bets, and the creditors did hold their hand until the race was over, when they were paid in full, and enough was left to re-establish Sir Robert in a fair position in life.'

SIGLAVY
Breeding for the Spanish Riding School

The world is a better place for the existence of the Lipizzaner horses at the Spanish Riding School in Vienna. The horses are extremely beautiful and astoundingly athletic, and the riders display an almost unbelievable level of horsemanship.

The origins of the Spanish Riding School as it is known today – 'Spanish' on account of the Andalusian breeding of the horses from way back in history – are to be found in the early eighteenth century, when Emperor Charles VI commissioned the building of what is now known as the Winter Riding School in 1729. Since then the school has been a byword for astonishing displays by horses and riders.

For centuries the key to the unique quality of the Spanish Riding School has been the breeding of the horses, at the Piber Federal Stud in western Styria, Austria. One of the original studs was at Lipizza, near Trieste – hence the name of the breed: Lipizzaner.

(While the majority of mature Lipizzaners are predominantly grey in colour, the greys are born dark, and acquire their pure white coats only as they grow older.)

The breed consists of six families: two Andalusian, two Neapolitan, one Frederiksborg, and one Arab, founded by the stallion Siglavy, born in 1810. This highly influential sire has been described as 'the exotic one with a past' as well as 'the drinker of the winds', and you can see why. Born in 1810 in Syria, he was moved to France before being purchased by Prince Karl Philipp von Schwarzenberg. In 1826 he was sold again, this time to the court stud farm to start a separate Lipizzan line which remains a key platform of the breeding programme. Siglavy also established a sire line for the Shagya Arabs.

But for all the niceties of the bloodlines, it is the sight of Lipizzaners in action which really activates the wow factor. Among the tours de force are:

- *Capriole:* the horse kicks out with his hind legs while leaping in the air from a static position;
- *Courbette:* the horse jumps forward on hind legs;
- *Levade:* the horse sits on his hind legs, with forelegs drawn up.

It is a mark of the huge esteem in which Lipizzaners are held that representatives of the breed have formed part of the inauguration parade for presidents Nixon, Carter, Reagan and Obama. The horses used on these occasions were from the Tempel Lipizzans, an outpost of the breed established by steel magnate Tempel Smith and his wife Esther, and based in Illinois.

SILVER
The Lone Ranger's horse

Thanks to the mysterious masked stranger and his magnificent white horse Silver, a wrong has been righted and justice has prevailed. The townsfolk are overwhelmed with gratitude but the masked man has no time to hang about. Others need assistance, and the Lone Ranger – clad in white, and wearing that trademark black mask to enhance his air of mystery – must be moving on. As his faithful Native American sidekick Tonto and Tonto's horse Scout join him, the Lone Ranger wheels Silver round for one last rear. He calls out the customary 'Hi-ho, Silver!' to his horse, and in a swirl of dust and the strains of Rossini's *William Tell* Overture the masked marvel is halfway to the next adventure before the baffled townsfolk have stopped scratching their ears and asking, 'Who was that man?'

They never find out, and nor do we. Tonto, who addresses his boss as 'Kemo sabe', knows – he's part of the complicated backstory – but he's not telling.

The Lone Ranger, one of the most durable of TV westerns, began life as a radio series in the 1930s, before moving to television. The programme ran from 1949 to 1957 in the USA, and from 1956 to 1962 in the United Kingdom.

We won't get an answer, but still we ask: who *was* that man?

SILVER BLAZE
Sherlock Holmes on top form

First published in the *Strand Magazine* in December 1892 and included in the collection *The Memoirs of Sherlock Holmes*, 'The Adventure of Silver Blaze' is deservedly one of the most popular Sherlock Holmes cases, with the great 'consulting detective' at the height of his powers.

The plot revolves around, in Dr Watson's crisp summary, 'the singular disappearance of the favourite for the Wessex Cup, and the tragic murder of its trainer'. Beyond observing that the fictitious Wessex Cup was run at Winchester (where there is no longer a racecourse), and that Silver Blaze's odds were 1/3 at the time of his disappearance, that plot will not be divulged here – though a measure of the intricacy of the story can be had from checking off such ingredients as curried mutton; limping sheep; powdered opium; a red and black silk cravat; a cataract knife; 'a costume of dove-coloured silk with ostrich feather trimming'; and, travelling on a train, how to gauge its speed when the telegraph poles are sixty yards apart. 'The calculation is a simple one,' observes Holmes.

Most famous ingredient of all is the celebrated stable dog, whose failure to react to the presence of a supposed stranger provides one of the most resonant exchanges in the whole Sherlock Holmes canon. Inspector Gregory of Scotland Yard asks Holmes:

'Is there any other point to which to which you would wish to draw my attention?'

'To the curious incident of the dog in the night-time.'

'The dog did nothing in the night-time.'

'That was the curious incident,' remarked Sherlock Holmes.

Arthur Conan Doyle, creator of Sherlock Holmes, readily acknowledged the paucity of his horse racing knowledge, writing in his 1924 memoir *Memories and Adventures*:

> Sometimes I have got upon dangerous ground where I have taken risks through my own want of knowledge of the correct atmosphere. I have, for example, never been a racing man, and yet I ventured to write 'Silver Blaze', in which the mystery depends upon the laws of training and racing. The story is all right, and Holmes may have been at the top of his form, but my ignorance cries aloud to heaven. I read an excellent and very damning criticism of the story in some sporting paper, written clearly by a man who *did* know, in which he explained the exact penalties which would have come upon every one concerned if they had acted as I described. Half would have been in jail and the other half warned off the Turf for ever.

In 1991 the Sherlock Holmes Society of London produced an audio recreation of the story, with the commentator Peter O'Sullevan calling the horses in the Wessex Cup. And the Society took its interest in 'Silver Blaze' even further by sponsoring a race entitled The Silver Blaze Wessex Cup at Kempton Park in May 2010.

SLEIPNIR

Eight-legged Norse horse

Sleipnir the eight-legged stallion; the grey horse ridden by the god Odin; the horse who could gallop over land and sea provides one of the most powerful images in Norse mythology.

The main planks for our knowledge of Sleipnir ('slippery' in Old Norse) are the *Poetic Edda*, compiled in the thirteenth century from earlier sources, and the *Prose Edda*, written in the thirteenth century by Snorri Sturluson. In both sources, Sleipnir is described as 'the best of horses'.

SPANKER

Not knowingly undersold

When a horse called Spanker was sold at auction at Epsom in 1820, the vendor's advertisement did not undersell the horse:

> On Saturday next will be sold by auction the strong, staunch, sturdy, stout, sound, safe, sinewy, serviceable, strapping, swift, smart, sightly, sprightly, spirited, sure-footed, well-sized, well-shaped, sorrell steed of superlative symmetry, styled Spanker, with small star and snip – free from, strain, spavin, string-halt, stranguary, staggers, scouring, strangles, sallenders [skin complaint], surfeit, starfoot, splint, scabs, scars, sores, shambling gait. He is neither spur-galled, sinew-shrunk, saddle-galled, shell-toothed, sling-gutted, surbated [with a bruised foot], short-winded, or shoulder slipped, and is sound in the swordpoint and stifle joint. Has neither sitfast, snaggle-teeth, sandcrack, staring coat, swelled sheath, nor scattered hoofs, nor is he sour, sulky, stubborn, or sullen

in temper; never slips, trips, stalks, starts, stops, shakes, snarvels, stumbles or stocks in the stable. Has a showy, stylish, switch tail.

History does not record how far this enterprise affected the price.

SPOTTED DOG
Bingo Little backs a loser

The writings of P.G. Wodehouse (1881–1975) are peppered with descriptions of horse racing, none more engaging than the story 'All's Well with Bingo' in *Eggs, Beans and Crumpets*, a collection of stories published in 1940.

Bingo Little, one of Bertie Wooster's chums at the Drones Club, has gone to the races in France, where he bets on a horse named Spotted Dog in the Prix Honoré Sauvan.

The result is not as Bingo would have wished. Spotted Dog finishes seventh – Wodehouse helpfully notes that there were seven runners – and some accommodation needs to be made between Bingo and the bookmaker with whom he has struck the bet.

The bookie is approached, and responds to Bingo's request for credit most encouragingly. Certainly, he says, and if Bingo wishes the bookie to wait for his money, he will wait – and suggests settling next Friday.

The delay Bingo has in mind is closer to a year, or eighteen months. He tries a few outside factors – 'the worldwide money shortage' is one – but the bookmaker is unimpressed, suggesting that the debt is settled according to his schedule rather than Bingo's, as he can't help recalling that some nasty accident has happened to every punter who has ever done him for money. He summons 'a frightful plugugly' named Erbut, whom he asks to remember Bingo's face. Erbut is certain he will. Good, says the bookmaker – 'Then about that money, Mr Little, we'll say Friday without fail, shall we?'

Elsewhere in the Wodehouse canon there is evidence of a proper knowledge of racing in his characters and in their creator. Jeeves, for example, is clearly very informed about the sport. 'One likes to keep *au courant* in these matters, sir,' he declares to Sir Roderick Carmoyle in *Ring for Jeeves*. 'It is, one might say, an essential part of one's education.'

And a happy combination of events meant that Bingo did not have to encounter the frightful plugugly Erbut again.

STEWBALL
The horse in song

> *Oh Stewball was a racehorse*
> *And I wish he were mine*
> *He never drank water*
> *He only drank wine.*

Stewball – sometimes spelled *Skewball*, or *Skuball*, or *Squball* – was an eighteenth-century racehorse whose achievements were first celebrated in a broadside dating from the 1780s. In the modern era the song has been recorded by such singers as Woody Guthrie, the Hollies, Peter, Paul and Mary, Steeleye Span, and Joan Baez. Other famous racehorses immortalised on vinyl include **PHAR LAP** (see entry) by Jack Lumsdaine; **ARKLE** (see entry) by Dominic Behan; **RED RUM** (see entry) by Christopher, Robin, Alice and Ted; while a tribute to Dawn Run (only horse to have won both the Champion Hurdle and Cheltenham Gold Cup) was sung by Foster and Allen.

Horses and racing also feature in music-hall songs.

There are songs about going to the Derby ('In My Little Donkey Cart' or 'In a Four-in-Hand', etc.), while 'Kempton Park', written by Harry Leighton in 1898 and performed by Pat Rafferty, tells how a misunderstanding threatens marital harmony:

> *When to my old girl I got married*
> *I gave up my dear pals and ways*
> *Life was all honey,*
> *But when I got money*
> *I longed for my old sporting days.*
> *Last week the post brought a letter*
> *From my racing pal, Micky Burke;*
> *Wrote Micky, 'Begorra!*
> *There's racing tomorrow,*
> *We'll go – Tell your wife you're at work.'*
> *Last night, when I went to my bed*
> *The wife found that letter which read*
> *(CHORUS:)*
> *I'll wait for you at the gate at Kempton Park.*
> *Won't we have a day?*
> *I've had a wire to say:*
> *Fair Mollie's in splendid form so keep it dark,*
> *And we'll have a fair old beano at Kempton Park.*

You can sense the storm clouds gathering – and sure enough, his wife's suspicions are fuelled when, in the second verse, she hears him talking about Mollie in his sleep.

The following day he sets off for the races:

The wife set out for Kempton soon after
And took up her stand by the gate.
I walked up so gaily,
Reading my daily,
When smash went her gamp on my pate!
'Now where's your Mollie?' she shouted,
As she held me quite fast by the hair.
Said I, 'Stop your folly,
If you want Fair Mollie,
She's only a race horse – a mare.'
Well we've settled the job out of court;
I tease her now only for sport.

And all join in the final chorus.

STIFF DICK and SORREL
Success then disaster for William III

Enthusiastic about horse racing and breeding, like many of his predecessors and successors, William III (1650–1702, reigned 1689–1702) liked to race his horses at Newmarket. Judged by one writer 'a consistent patron of the Turf and a grand man for a wager', William raced such good horses as Turk, Cupid and Cricket, and in April 1698 pitched his horse Stiff Dick against Careless, owned by the Marquess of Wharton and considered the best horse in England. To general surprise, the lightly weighted Stiff Dick narrowly beat his rival.

In 1702 William was riding Sorrel when his horse stumbled over a molehill, dumping his royal rider, who subsequently succumbed to pneumonia. William was succeeded by Queen

Anne, a great devotee of hunting (despite her girth) and horse racing, founding Ascot racecourse in 1711.

STORM CAT
Thoroughbred stallion with an unusual by-product

A high-class racehorse in the USA, Storm Cat found his true metier in the breeding shed, where he became a hugely influential stallion – so influential, indeed, that his manure was sent to the Campbell's Soup Company for use in the manufacture of mushroom soup. (According to *Stud: Adventures in Breeding* by Kevin Conley (2002), that is.)

STREIFF
In the fog of war

The battle of Lützen between Sweden and the Holy Roman Empire in November 1632 was one of the most significant clashes of the Thirty Years War, notable not merely for costing the life of the Swedish king Gustavus Adolphus, but for immortalising a horse named Streiff.

On a morning thick with swirling fog, Gustavus Adolphus led the Swedish forces from the back of Streiff, a horse of Oldenburg blood – until, when leading a cavalry charge around 1 p.m., the king was knocked out of the saddle and killed.

Even as the king was struck, Streiff himself took a direct hit in the neck and keeled over. He managed to stand up and staggered around in vain search of Gustavus Adolphus, eventually picking his way through the fog to a position behind his own lines. The sight of a wounded horse bearing an empty saddle told its own story. The Swedish forces re-formed, and overran the enemy.

Gustavus Adolphus had not survived, but Streiff had, and formed part of the procession which accompanied Gustavus Adolphus's body through northern Germany after the battle.

After Streiff died in 1633 – less than a year after the battle of Lützen – his hide was displayed in the Royal Armoury in Stockholm, where it remains.

THE CHASE
Twelve-year-old Lester Piggott's first winner

On 7 April 1948 a cherub-faced schoolboy named Lester Piggott, son of trainer Keith Piggott, had his first race in public at the age of twelve. The race was a humble apprentice handicap at Salisbury, and Piggott's mount, a three-year-old filly named The Chase and trained by his father, finished unplaced.

'She was pretty ordinary, really,' he recalled decades later. 'Nice and quiet' – and thus a suitably safe conveyance for a young man embarking on his riding career.

Young Lester had five more losing rides – three of them on The Chase – before going up to Haydock Park in Lancashire to ride the filly in the Wigan Lane Selling Handicap on 18 August 1948.

By happy chance, the day of Lester Piggott's first winner was to coincide with the day of Donald Bradman's final Test match appearance, Australia having beaten England in the morning. One sporting icon was leaving the stage, even as another walked out of the wings.

The Chase started at 10/1 for the Wigan Lane seller, and hit the front with a quarter of a mile to race, her young jockey pushing her home.

But there was a twist to come.

Among The Chase's rivals was Prompt Corner, ridden by Davy Jones. In racing parlance, Prompt Corner was 'not off': that is, not intended to win, in order to deceive the handicapper. Lester recalled: 'As we went past Prompt Corner, Davy Jones was urging me on, yelling, "Go on! Go on!" at me. I suppose you could draw your own conclusions from that.'

And Davy Jones later commented: 'I wasn't fancied. Lester might say I wasn't trying, but I wasn't fancied - which was different!'

The victory of the twelve-year-old wunderkind brought headlines in the national press, but Lester did not ride his second winner until just over a year later. He was understandably short of opportunities since he was still at school, but gradually the flood gates opened further, and by the early 1950s he was hailed as a riding phenomenon.

The bare bones tell the story of the career.

He was champion apprentice twice and champion jockey eleven times. He won thirty English Classics (a record), nine of which came in the Derby at Epsom (also a record): Never Say Die (1954), followed by Crepello, St Paddy, Sir Ivor, NIJINSKY, Roberto, Empery, The Minstrel and Teenoso (1983).

He rode 116 winners at Royal Ascot – streets ahead of any

other jockey – including the Gold Cup eleven times. He won the King George VI and Queen Elizabeth Stakes seven times; Prix de l'Arc de Triomphe three times; and sixteen Irish Classic victories, which included the Irish Derby five times – notably on **SHERGAR** in 1981.

He retired in 1985 to start a training career, but that was brought to a shuddering halt by conviction for tax fraud in 1987. Released a year and a day after commencing his prison sentence, he seemed to be taking things very quietly – then astonished the sporting world by returning to the saddle a few weeks short of his fifty-fifth birthday. A mere twelve days after his return, he produced the ride of his life to win the Breeders' Cup Mile at Belmont Park, New York, on Royal Academy – trained by Vincent O'Brien, for whom he had ridden so many great horses over several decades.

His last domestic winner was Palacegate Jack at Haydock Park in October 1994.

In all he rode 4,493 winners on the Flat in Great Britain, plus 800-odd overseas (nobody has yet arrived at the exact figure) and twenty hurdle races (from fifty-nine).

As for The Chase, who set in motion the greatest riding career of all, she was sold for 330 guineas (£346.50) at the post-race auction following the Wigan Lane Selling Handicap, and moved to a new trainer.

But she has not been forgotten. The coincidence of Lester Piggott's first and last domestic winners both coming at Haydock Park led his wife Susan to commission from the leading equine sculptor Willie Newton a dramatic bronze illustrating The Chase, ridden by young Lester at the age of twelve, upsides Palacegate Jack, ridden by the fifty-five-year-old Lester.

Before we enthuse too much about the horse who won only once in her life and just happened to be the right horse at the right time to secure her place in history, bear in mind how Lester Piggott himself evaluates that famous occasion: 'It was just the start of the job, really, wasn't it? That's all.'

THE PIEBALD
National Velvet's National 'winner'

Enid Bagnold's novel *National Velvet*, published in 1935, chronicles how Velvet Brown – farmer's daughter, fourteen years old and horse-mad – buys a raffle ticket for a shilling (5p in modern money) and acquires a gelding, described by stable-hand Mi Taylor as part carthorse and part Arab.

Velvet becomes obsessed by the prospect of training 'Pie' for the Grand National at Aintree and riding him in the race, despite the fact that female jockeys were ineligible. She will get round that detail by disguising herself.

Guess what: she rides in the big race and she wins. Her identity is quickly uncovered and she is disqualified, though the authorities decline to take further action against her.

The movie of *National Velvet*, starring a youthful Elizabeth Taylor as Velvet ('Every day I pray to God to give me horses!') and Micky Rooney as Mi Taylor, came out in 1944 and has remained a popular favourite, which is more than can be said of *International Velvet*, released in 1978 as a sequel to the earlier film. In the 1944 movie, the horse is not piebald (Thoroughbreds cannot be of that black and white colour); he is called 'Pie' as an abbreviation of 'Pirate'. In the same film, much of the Grand National footage was staged on a golf course in Pasadena.

The politician Baroness Williams of Crosby – Shirley Williams – screen-tested for the part of Velvet Brown in the 1944 movie after she had been evacuated to the USA as a child during the Second World War. 'I don't think I was cut out to be a film actress,' she confessed when interviewed by Michael Parkinson on BBC Radio 4's *Desert Island Discs*. 'I doubt if my looks would have lasted, and maybe they weren't appropriate anyway.' She recalled how both she and a young actress named Elizabeth Taylor had screen tests, 'and Betty Taylor, by some strange fluke, actually won, and of course set off on a great film career'.

THROWAWAY
Racehorse immortalised in James Joyce classic

James Joyce's novel *Ulysses*, published in 1922, is set in Dublin on a single day in June which is still commemorated as 'Bloomsday' after the novel's main character, Leopold Bloom.

In 1904 that day coincided with the running of the Gold Cup, flagship race of the prestigious Royal Ascot meeting, which that year featured the great five-year-old mare Sceptre, who in 1902 had won four of the five English Classic races, missing out only on the Derby.

A scene in the novel graphically describes how Bloom and his friends Lenehan and Phyllis experience the famous race. O'Madden Burke, another friend, has backed Sceptre, partly because she is ridden by his near-namesake, the jockey Otto Madden. Bloom describes the scene:

> Madden had lost five drachmas on Sceptre for a whim of
> the rider's name: Lenehan as much more. He told them of

the race. The flag fell and, huuh, off, scamper, the mare ran out freshly with O. Madden up. She was leading the field: all hearts were beating. Even Phyllis could not contain herself. She waved her scarf and shouted: Huzzah! Sceptre wins! But in the straight on the run home when all were in close order the dark horse Throwaway drew level, reached, outstripped her. All was lost now. Phyllis was silent: her eyes were sad anemones. Juno, she cried, I am undone. But her lover consoled her and brought her a bright casket of gold in which lay some oval sugarplums which she partook. A tear fell: one only. A whacking fine whip, said Lenehan, is W. Lane. Four winners yesterday and three today. What rider is like him? Mount him on the camel or the boisterous buffalo the victory in a hack canter is still his. But let us bear it as is the ancient wont. Mercy on the luckless! Poor Sceptre! he said with a light sigh. She is not the filly that she was. Never, by this hand, shall we behold such another.

TOPPER

Hopalong Cassidy's horse

Hopalong Cassidy, destined to become one of the most popular of the genial, wrong-righting, television-cowboy genre, was created by Clarence E. Mulford, the first fruit of whose labours was the 1904 story 'The Fight at Buckskin'. Hoppy's original personality was that of a brusque manner and a wooden leg, which gives him a limp – hence 'Hopalong'.

By the time that Hoppy had started appearing in films in the mid-1930s, he had smartened himself up, and with clean-cut actor William Boyd taking the lead role, so the character had been transformed. Even his horse – the snow-white stallion Topper – was noticeably well turned out.

There were sixty-six Hopalong Cassidy movies, and meanwhile Hoppy was establishing a career in television. Boyd cannily bought the rights to his old films, and reaped the reward when his fictitious character proved highly popular on the new medium. Radio followed, plus a wave of commercial merchandising aimed at the children who formed the majority of Hoppy's audience.

William Boyd died in 1972.

TOSCA, PRINCE HAL and FLANAGAN
Pat Smythe's great showjumpers

Tosca was one of the best and most popular showjumping mares of the 1950s, when ridden by her owner Pat Smythe (later Pat Koechlin-Smythe). Together they won the Northern Championship in 1952 and 1954, the Midland and South of England Championships in 1952, the Ladies National and West of England Championships in 1953, and the Victor Ludorum at the Horse of the Year Show in 1954. In addition, they formed part of the British team in Prix des Nations events in 1952 and 1953.

Prince Hal won major competitions all over the world, including the Daily Mail Cup at the Royal International Horse Show at the White City in 1955 and 1957, and the Prix des Nations in 1953 – though that tally is dwarfed by Pat Smythe winning the Prix des Nations no fewer than eight times on Flanagan. She was the first woman to compete in a showjumping event at the Olympic Games, riding Flanagan and helping the British team to the bronze medal at Stockholm in 1956.

Showjumping is a sport with more subtlety than immediately meets the eye, and publication in 1952 of Pat Smythe's autobiography *Jump for Joy* – one of the best-selling sports books of its generation, commercial success reflecting the huge popularity of its author – gave her the opportunity to provide an illuminating glimpse of the level of thought required at the highest reaches of her sport.

Good show jumpers, she wrote, are like good athletes who love their sport, and as with human athletes, tend to have a temperament to match the athletic ability.

For Smythe, one of the finest experiences has been to compare the very different qualities of Tosca and Prince Hal: the former in her element in the open air, the latter much more effective in an inside arena. It is, she declares, a question of the two horses' different sorts of boldness: Hal, the excitable Thoroughbred who demands freedom and the right to assume complete control as opposed to Tosca, 'who is ultra-careful, hates touching a fence, and on the indoor course often becomes over-anxious.'

Pat Smythe – who in addition to her show-jumping achievements rode the winners of three point-to-points – died in 1996. A couple of days later a correspondent to *The Times* wrote: 'When reading her obituary, I was struck by her determination and zest for life in all the situations in which she found herself – perhaps a lesion for the heroes and heroines of the children of today. She was a true British sportswoman and is a great loss to a far wider world than the horsy one which she loved and graced for so long.'

TRAVELLER
Robert E. Lee's favourite horse

Robert E. Lee (1807–1870) was acknowledged to be one of the great Confederate generals of the American Civil War, and as would be expected of a military figure of that status, many well-known horses punctuate his biography. These include the mare Lucy Long (who continued to live with the Lee family after the end of the war, and died at the age of thirty-three) and the sorrel horse Ajax (who also remained with the Lee family after the war).

But Lee's favourite horse was Traveller. Foaled in what is now West Virginia in 1857, the iron-grey went through several owners (and names) before being sold to Lee and being renamed by his new master.

When Mary Lee's cousin Markie Williams approached the general with a request to paint Traveller, Lee's response was a moving summary of what made this horse special:

> If I was an artist like you, I should draw a true picture of Traveller; representing his fine proportions, muscular figure, deep chest, short back, strong haunches, flat legs, small head, broad forehead, delicate ears, quick eye, small feet, and black mane and tail.
>
> Such a picture would inspire a poet, whose genius could then depict his worth, and describe his endurance of toil, hunger, thirst, heat and cold; and the dangers and suffering through which he had passed. He could dilate upon his sagacity and affection, and his invariable response to every wish of his rider. He might even imagine his thoughts through the long-marches and days of the battle through which he has passed. But I am no artist, Markie,

and therefore can only say he is a Confederate grey.

Traveller outlived Lee, and his remains were initially buried next to the Lee Chapel – a measure of the regard in which this horse was held.

TRIGGER (1)
Roy Rogers' horse

Roy Rogers (1911–1998) was the most popular of the singing-cowboy film stars of the mid-twentieth century, and the palomino stallion Trigger became an indelible part of the Roy Rogers persona. (Roy's sidekick was Dale Evans, whose horse was Buttermilk.)

When Rogers first rode Trigger, he was impressed by the horse's balance and responsiveness – 'He could turn on a dime and give you some change' – and the combination first performed together in the movie *Under Western Stars* in 1938. In all, Trigger served Roy Rogers in more than eighty films, plus 101 episodes of the Rogers television series.

Trigger died at the age of thirty in 1965. His body was stuffed and, posed rearing on his hind legs, displayed at the Roy Rogers and Dale Evans Museum in Branson, Missouri (now closed down). In July 2010 his stuffed incarnation was offered at auction by Christie's in New York and sold for US$266,500 along with Roy's dog Bullet for US$35,000.

TRIGGER (2)
Ernie's horse

'Ernie (the Fastest Milkman in the West)', a 1971 Christmas

number 1 chart hit for comedian Benny Hill, describes the intense rivalry between milkman Ernie and baker Two-Ton Ted from Teddington for the affections of a widow named Sue.

Trigger makes his appearance as the song reaches its climax. Ted, enraged to see that Ernie has been closeted with Sue all afternoon, stomps across to the milkman's cart – 'and he didn't half kick his horse'.

When Ernie emerges from Sue's house, a duel ensues, and Ernie is killed by a stale pork pie hitting him in the eye – though he exacts his revenge by haunting Sue and Ted from beyond the grave.

The model for this Trigger was a mare named Daisy, who pulled the milk cart driven by the young Alfie (later Benny) Hill in Eastleigh, Hampshire, in the early 1940s. Seventeen-year-old Alfie was noted by his employers for his skill at handling difficult horses, Daisy among them. For his part, as Alfie tore into Market Street at the gallop, bottles jingling and cart screeching round the corners, he would fantasise that he was galloping into Dodge City.

'Ernie' was one of the record choices of then Leader of the Opposition David Cameron when he appeared on the Radio 4 programme *Desert Island Discs* in May 2006. Cameron claimed that 'Ernie' was the only song which he knew off by heart, and supported that claim by reciting the first few lines.

UCHCHAIHSHRAVAS
Seven-headed horse

In Hindu mythology, Uchchaihshravas is the seven-headed flying horse born during the churning of the milk ocean, and is acknowledged to be the finest of horses.

UNICORN
Horned mythical and heraldic beast

The unicorn, a sort of smorgasbord of body parts, has a very long history, having been first mentioned in literature around 400 BCE. Its shape and accoutrements are subject to variation, but the standard list includes: the head and body of a horse; legs of a buck; tail of a lion; cloven hooves; goat-like beard (optional); and a single spiralling horn emerging from its forehead.

It is that last feature which has attracted such attention for so long, and the horn has been claimed to have special powers – notably that, if dipped into a liquid, it could detect poison.

A fourteenth-century account describes the unicorn in this way:

> The unicorn has but one horn in the middle of its forehead. It is the only animal that ventures to attack the elephant; and so sharp is the nail of its foot, that with one blow it can rip the belly of the beast. Hunters can catch the unicorn only by placing a young virgin in his haunts. No sooner does he see the damsel, than he runs towards her, and lies down at her feet, and suffers himself to be captured by the hunters. The unicorn represents Jesus Christ, who took on him our nature in the virgin's womb, was betrayed by the Jews and delivered into the hands of Pontius Pilate. Its one horn signifies the Gospel of Truth.

There are zillions of unicorns in the **MY LITTLE PONY** range.

UFFINGTON WHITE HORSE
Oldest of the hillside white horses

Of the numerous white horses carved into the UK landscape, some are more spectacular than others. But the most astonishing of all of them – and the oldest – is the Uffington White Horse near Wantage, now in Oxfordshire (in Berkshire until county boundary changes in 1972).

There is no written confirmation of its existence before the twelfth century, no descriptive account until the sixteenth century and no proper likeness until the eighteenth.

Archaeological analysis in recent times has established that the Uffington White Horse dates back to the Bronze Age, but the nature of its origin and meaning remains baffling. Possibilities include the White Horse as tribal banner; as battle memorial; as symbol of a cult; and even, in the absence of alternative suggestions, as a primeval piece of advertisement put there by a horse trader. Local tradition has it that the white horse was the emblem of King Alfred, who was born in Wantage, and that he had the horse figure carved to celebrate his beating the Danes at the battle of Ashdown in 871 – which theory does not stand up since the use of modern archaeological evidence.

G.K. Chesterton wrote, in 'The Ballad of the White Horse':

> *Before the gods that made the gods*
> *Had seen their sunrise pass,*
> *The White Horse of the White Horse Vale*
> *Was cut out of the grass.*

The White Horse needs regular maintenance, and has been fortunate in attracting the services of local volunteers to preserve that extraordinary figure.

Other notable landscape white horses include the one at Osmington, near Weymouth, with George III astride the horse; the Westbury White Horse and Cherhill White Horse, both in Wiltshire; the Kilburn White Horse in North Yorkshire; and the Mormond White Horse in Aberdeenshire.

VESUVIUS
Gift horse

When in 2017 President Macron of France visited China, he presented to his host Xi Jinping the gift of an eight-year-old horse named Vesuvius – the perfect return gift after the Chinese premier had expressed his admiration for the horses of the Republican Guard in France when he visited Paris in 2014.

An Élysée official declared that the gift 'mattered a lot for the president, even if it was very complicated to import a horse for sanitary reasons. It's a symbol of French excellence.'

The gift to Xi Jinping was part of a long tradition of diplomacy, in which horses have played a part. For example, King Abdul Aziz al-Saud of Saudi Arabia presented a horse named Tarfa to George VI to mark his coronation in 1937.

And Princess Elizabeth – later Queen Elizabeth II – received a filly foal from the then Aga Khan on her marriage to Prince Philip in 1947. The filly was named Astrakhan, and provided her new owner with her first victory on the Flat when winning at Hurst Park in April 1950.

VIPER (plus ARSENIC and TRAVAIL)
Horses at Cold Comfort Farm

In Stella Gibbons's great comic novel *Cold Comfort Farm*, published in 1952, the buggy used by the Starkadders – a dysfunctional family to end all dysfunctional families – is pulled by a 'vicious gelding' named Viper. Arsenic and Travail are the ploughing team.

We first encounter Arsenic and Travail ploughing a field – to the encouraging cries of 'Upidee, Travail! Ho, there, Arsenic! Jug-jug!' – while Viper is usually in the charge of Adam Lambsbreath, the ancient farm hand.

When Viper is dispatched to the station at Howling to collect Flora Poste from London, Adam pulls up the horse in the nick of time just as he is about to canter through the entrance to the booking hall. When Viper has the limelight, mayhem is never far behind – such as when the horse is being prepared for a ride:

> Viper, the great gelding, was harnessed to the trap; and
> Adam, who had been called from the cowshed to get the
> brute between the shafts, was being swung up and down in
> the air as he hung on to the reins.
>
> The great beast, nineteen hands high, jerked his head
> wickedly, and Adam's frail body flew up into the darkness

beyond the circles of grave, gold light painted by the mog's-lanthorn, and was lost to sight.

Then down he came again, a twisted grey moth falling into the light as Viper thrust his head down to snuff the reeking straw about his feet . . .

As Amos struck Viper on the shanks and the beast jerked his head as though he had been shot, Adam was flung out of the circle of light into the thick darkness, and was seen no more.

WALLACE THE GREAT
Rescue mule takes on the British equestrian establishment

Wallace the Great is a mule. There is no debate about that. But he is a mule with a special ability – one denied to most mules: he excels at dressage, that branch of equestrianism which has been described as '*Strictly Come Dancing* with horses'.

In 2017 he entered his first dressage competition – and won. His fame rapidly spreading, in 2019 he was invited to display his skills at the Festival of British Eventing at Gatcombe Park. But the International Federation for Equestrian Sports (FEI) threatened to ban him from competition, on the grounds that he is a mule, and not a horse, and dressage is for horses.

WARRIOR
'The horse the Germans can't kill'

Not many horses have their deaths written up in the national press, and when *The Times* of 5 April 1941 carried a column headed, 'My Horse Warrior: Death of a Well-known Charger', it was an appropriate farewell to a famous horse.

Bred by his owner Jack Seely, the 'Galloper Jack' of military-history fame, Warrior was born on the Isle of Wight in 1908. Six years later he engaged with the First World War, landing in Le Havre to join the Allies on the Western Front. After returning to England in spring 1915, Warrior crossed the English Channel again to join the Canadian cavalry. He played an active role in many of the major actions of the war: in the trenches near Ypres; at Mons and the battle of the Somme; at Paschendaele; and in the front line at Cambrai. In 1918 he carried Seely in the charge at Moreuil, and stayed in France with General Patterson after his owner had been gassed. Despite his length of service the horse was never seriously injured, though he was twice buried while under bombardment. Fittingly, the Canadians called him 'The horse the Germans can't kill'.

Seely himself later summed up his great partner:

> His escapes were quite wonderful. Again and again he survived when death seemed certain and, indeed, befell all his neighbours. It was not all hazard; sometimes it was due to his intelligence. I have seen him, even when a shell has burst within a few feet, stand still without a tremor – just turn his head and, unconcerned, look at the smoke of the burst.

At the end of hostilities Warrior retired to the Seelys' home,

Mottistone Manor. In July 1919 he took part in the Victory Parade in Hyde Park, and he later appeared in a parade of veteran warhorses at what was then called the Horse Show at Olympia. More remarkable, he took part in – and won – the lightweight race at the Isle of Wight point-to-point in 1922.

Seely's book *My Horse Warrior* was published in 1934, with exquisite illustrations by his friend Alfred Munnings (and was reissued in 2011 with an introduction by Seely's grandson, the journalist and television presenter Brough Scott).

Warrior's reputation had steadily risen over the years, and in retirement his bravery had continued to be recorded. Seely – who became Lord Mottistone – would occasionally write to the press to keep the horse's fans up to date. His last bulletin was sent in May 1938, when Seely reported that Warrior and he had cantered together over Mottistone Downs – 'greatly rejoicing, our united ages being exactly 100 years'.

Close to the end of *My Horse Warrior*, his owner muses:

> I am persuaded that the real reason why he has thus impressed his personality and character upon all those who have been brought into contact with him, in peace and in war, is the fact that he has never been ill-treated, never badly used, never beaten when he was doing his best.
>
> The soul of a horse is a great and loyal soul, quite unspoiled by the chances and changes of human kind. Above all, it is a courageous soul, and an affectionate soul. But let there be one cruel blow from a grown-up man, and you have ruined the horse's fine soul and spirit for ever.

Warrior died peacefully at Mottistone in April 1941, at the age of thirty-two.

WHISTLEJACKET
Familiar but always breath-taking horse portrait

Every time you see the portrait of Whistlejacket, painted in 1762, the effect is the same: jaw-dropping amazement at the scale, the motion, the raw power of George Stubbs's most famous painting, now in the National Gallery in London. Well over life-size, it depicts a staring-eyed Whistlejacket, a deep chestnut but with flaxen mane and tail which make the horse look almost palomino.

The authors of the catalogue of the extensive Stubbs exhibition which opened at the Tate Gallery (now Tate Britain) in January 1985 found the Whistlejacket portrait irresistible:

> This astonishing image has never lost its power to compel attention. Its impressiveness is by no means merely a factor of size (John Wootton has painted even larger portraits of horses): it is, rather, a question of authoritativeness. There can be no doubt that the artist who modelled this horse knew the structure and function of every muscle and bone in its body.

It is easy to forget, in all the wowing, that Whistlejacket was a real racehorse – and a good one at that.

Foaled in 1749, he raced for most of his career in the ownership of his breeder Sir William Middleton, for whom he won ten of his twelve races. Before the 1757 season Middleton sold the horse to the Marquess of Rockingham, for whom he ran five more races, of which he won three more times, including a match race at York against Brutus for the huge stake of two thousand guineas in August 1759. After that race he was retired from the track, having won thirteen of his seventeen races, including two walkovers. He was then retired to stud.

By the late eighteenth century, George Stubbs (1724–1806) was the most eminent equine painter of his age, having laid the foundations of his genius with relentless study of horse's carcasses – studies brought into the open with publication of *Anatomy of the Horse* in 1766, as well as painting portraits of such great champions as ECLIPSE and Gimcrack, and the wonderful 'Racehorses Exercising on the Downs at Goodwood' (1760).

In 1762 the Marquess of Rockingham wanted a portrait of his horse Whistlejacket, and Stubbs was, to coin a phrase, the 'go-to man'.

According to the catalogue for the Tate exhibition, Whistlejacket was not an easy sitter, a view supported by a near-contemporary memoir of Stubbs written by Ozias Humphry:

> A stable boy was as usual leading Whistlejacket backwards and forwards in front of a long range of stables when Stubbs removed the picture from his easel and placed it against the stable-wall 'to view the effect of it, and was scumbling and glazing it here and there'. Whistlejacket, suddenly catching sight for the first time of his own image, began to 'stare and look wildly at the picture, endeavouring to get at it, to fight and to kick it. Stubbs had to come to the stable boy's aid and pummel Whistlejacket with his palette and Mahl stick before the horse could be quietened and led away.

Why does Whistlejacket have no rider in the portrait? There has long been speculation that the horse was going to be ridden by George III, until political differences came between Rockingham and the King, and Whistlejacket was deliberately left in splendid isolation. In any case, the lack of human or landscape elements forces the viewer to concentrate all attention on the horse himself.

The portrait passed down generations of the Rockingham family – it was loaned to Kenwood House in Hampstead, London, from 1971 to 1981 – before being acquired by the nation, following a public appeal.

(A concoction mixing treacle and gin, whistlejacket is – understandably – considered an efficacious treatment for colds.)

XENOPHON

Horseman supreme

Historian, military leader and student as well as contemporary of Socrates, Xenophon (circa 444–365 BCE) is arguably the most influential horseman in history, with works such as *The Art of Horsemanship* still proving instructive centuries after their composition.

This passage, for example, describes priorities when buying a horse:

> In the case of an unbroken colt, of course his frame is what you must test; as for spirit, no very sure signs of that are offered by an animal that has never yet been mounted. And in his frame, the first things which I say you ought to look at are his feet. Just as a house would be good for nothing

if it were very handsome above but lacked the proper
foundations, so too a war-horse, even if all his other points
were fine, would yet be good for nothing if he had bad feet;
for he could not use a single one of his five points.

Or the demeanour of a young horse going off to be 'broken':

See to it that the colt be kind, used to the hand, and fond of
men when he is put out to the horse-breaker. He is generally
made so at home and by the groom, if the man knows how to
manage so that solitude means to the colt hunger and thirst
and teasing horseflies, while food, drink and relief from pain
come from man. For if this be done, colts must not only love
men, but even long for them.

Then, too, the horse should be stroked in the places
which he most likes to have handled; that is, where the
hair is thickest, and where he is least able to help himself if
anything hurts him.

The groom should also be directed to lead him through
crowds, and to make him familiar with all sorts of sights and
all sorts of noises. Whenever the colt is frightened at any of
them, he should be taught, not by irritating but by soothing
him, that there is nothing to fear.

It seems to me that this is enough to tell the amateur to do
in the matter of horse-breaking.

And Xenophon is a man of very strong practical opinions:

Washing down of the legs is a thing I absolutely forbid; it
does no good – on the contrary, daily washing is bad for the
hoofs. And washing under the belly should be done very
sparingly; it worries the horse more than washing anywhere
else, and the cleaner these parts are made, the more they

attract things under the belly that would torment it.

And no matter what pains one has spent on it, the horse is no sooner led out than it gets exactly as dirty as before. These parts, then, should be let alone; and as for the legs, rubbing with the mere hand is quite enough.

XERXES

One of John Jorrocks's horses

R.S. Surtees (1805–1864) is little read these days, his world dominated by foxhunting and rural shenanigans proving increasingly alien to the modern sensibility. His collection *Jorrocks's Jaunts and Jollities*, published in 1838, charts the fun had by the jovial sporting cockney grocer John Jorrocks, one of whose horses is named Xerxes. Another Jorrocks horse is called Arterxerxes – named thus because, when the two horses were driven to the meet in tandem, Xerxes was in front, and Arterxerxes behind – that is, he was 'Arter' Xerxes. Geddit?

YEAR OF THE HORSE
. . . in Chinese astrology

The horse is the seventh of the twelve-year cycle of creatures which shapes the Chinese calendar. (The others are dog, tiger, goat, pig, rabbit, snake, ox, rooster, dragon, monkey and rat.) The year commences in late January or early/mid-February, and in the foreseeable future the Years of the Horse are 2026, 2038, 2050, 2062 and 2074.

Much of the apparatus of Chinese astrology is impenetrable to non-believers, but some is worth bearing in mind. For example, if you are going to be born in the Year of the Horse, the time to emerge is during the two hours between 11 p.m. and 1 a.m. – oh, and be born in the June of the Year of the Horse if you can so arrange matters.

The Horse-born are, to quote one manual, 'popular,

friendly, carefree, optimistic, pleasure-seeking, imaginative, inquisitive, capable, practical, energetic, impulsive'. Career preferences? Business, agriculture and art are especially worth considering. Romance? Amorous and faithful. And as for well-known Horse-born celebrities, Nelson Mandela (born in 1918) and Paul McCartney (1942) set the bar pretty high.

ZAD-ER-RAKIB
. . . and the Arabians

Widely considered the most beautiful of all horse breeds, the Arab has a history shrouded in myth, legend and tradition. Archaeological excavations have demonstrated the existence of Arab horses in the Saudi Arabian deserts at least 3,000 years before the birth of Christ.

Alternative tradition has it that the Arab traces back to the five mares of Muhammad who were the first to reach Mecca from eighty-five dispatched by the Prophet to bring news of a great military victory.

After the death of Muhammad in 632, Arabian tribes conquered the area between Egypt and Persia, and the influence of the Arab horse started to spread far afield, to Spain and to France.

The great proponents of Arab breeding in Britain were Wilfred Scawen Blunt and his wife Anne, who in the late 1870s brought a number of horses from the northern Arabian deserts to their Crabbet Stud in Sussex.

In summary, the characteristics of the Arab horse are:

- head small and profile concave;
- eyes very large and circular;
- forehead broad;
- mouth longer than in ordinary horses;
- ears small;
- neck arched;
- chest broad and deep;
- body well ribbed up;
- quarters broad;
- tail set on a level with the back and carried high;
- legs strong;
- pasterns springy;
- feet hard and round;
- action: free at trot and walk.

The Arab skeleton has features unique to the breed: seventeen ribs on each side (other horses have eighteen); five lumbar vertebrae (other horses have six); and sixteen tail vertebrae (other horses have eighteen).

Arab influence on other horse and pony breeds has been immense, and wherever its blood has gone it has brought quality to that breed. Some familiar breeds proclaim the Arab infusion through the excellence of the horse's physique. The Thoroughbred is the most significant example, while breeds such as the Shagya, Lipizzaner, Orlov, Alter-Real and Akhal-

Teke owe a great deal to the Arab influence, as do draught breeds such as Percheron and Boulannais.

Zad-er-Rakib was one of King Solomon's horses, and there is a legend that the original bloodlines of all Arab stallions derive from this one horse.

ZEBRA CROSSINGS
Of zebroids and zonkeys

Of the six species of modern equid, three are zebras: the Plains zebra, Grévy's zebra and Mountain zebra. See **EQUUS CABALLUS**.

And various matings have set the challenge of coining new names for new combinations. For example:

- **Zebroid** for the offspring of a zebra and any other equine;
- **Zonkey** for the offspring of a zebra and donkey.

ZIPPY CHIPPY
Famous loser

If **ELSICH** and his fellows are among the great losers in British racing history, the USA has Zippy Chippy.

Foaled in 1991 and reportedly acquired by owner/trainer Felix Monserrate in exchange for an '88 Ford truck, Zippy Chippy had a racing record with a nice roundness to it: 100 races and no wins, though he did net over $30,000 in place money.

Zippy Chippy had his quirks, prominent among which was to miss the break at the start of a race. The authorities at his home track, Finger Lakes, New York, had the patience of saints but eventually could take no more. Losing is not really what horse racing is about, and in 1998 he was banned from competing at Finger Lakes.

But he continued running elsewhere, and reached the landmark century at the Northampton Fair in September 2004, after which he was retired from racing, and spent some time serving as an outrider's pony back at Finger Lakes.

Closer to the spirit of the circus ring than the racecourse, Monserrate set up all manner of novelty competitions for his horse – taking on a minor league baseball player over forty yards, for example, or running a match race against a harness horse – and Zippy Chippy became such a celebrity that in 2000 he was included in a list of the nation's 'Most Interesting Characters' in *People* magazine.

On retirement from competition, Zippy Chippy became a celebrity inmate at the Old Friends centre at Cabin Creek, New York: a winner, of a sort, at last.

Acknowledgements

Many people have helped with this book. Ranked alphabetically, as is the main text, they are: Brian Alderson; Professor Richard Beadle; Liam Binns of KopyRite; Suzanne Bridson; Nick Clee; Richard Fisher; Frances and George Goodwin; Tim Hailstone; Maureen Hammond; David Heighway; the late Dr Peter Linehan; Arianna Magee; Donald McRae; Rebecca Mundy; David Murphy; Anne O'Brien; Chris Pitt; Graham Sharpe; Michael Tanner; and Professor Tony Wright. Apologies for inadvertent omissions.

Particular thanks are due to Mary Thompson of the Fred W. Smith National Library for the Study of George Washington in Washington DC, for extensive information and for permission to quote from the excellent resources of the library ; to Brough Scott, for permission to quote from his grandfather's book *My Horse Warrior*; to the tireless Tim Cox, for the wonder that is the Cox Library; and to David Ashforth, who went well beyond the call of friendship to come up with all sorts of insights – including the fact that the stuffed body of Roy Rogers' horse Trigger was sold to the man who also bought Rogers' dog Bullet.

I have long wanted to publish a book with the legendary editor Alan Samson, while there is only one suitable word for Lucinda McNeile and Ellie Freedman at Weidenfeld & Nicolson: incomparable.

Index of main entries

(Some horses appear under more than one heading.)